❧❧❧❧❧❧❧❧❧❧❧❧❧❧❧❧❧❧❧❧❧❧❧❧❧

IRISH STATESMAN AND REBEL:

The Two Lives of Eamon De Valera

OTHER BOOKS BY BILL SEVERN

Adlai Stevenson:
  Citizen of the World
Frontier President:
  The Life of James K. Polk
Hand in Glove
Here's Your Hat
If the Shoe Fits
In Lincoln's Footsteps:
  The Life of Andrew Johnson
John Marshall
  The Man Who Made the Court Supreme
Magic and Magicians
Magic Comedy:
  Tricks, Skits and Clowning
Magic in Your Pockets
Magic Shows You Can Give
Magic Wherever You Are
Magic with Paper
Packs of Fun
People Words
Place Words
Rope Roundup:
  The Lore and Craft of Ropes and Roping
Samuel J. Tilden
  And the Stolen Election
Story of the Human Voice
Teacher, Soldier, President:
  The Life of James A. Garfield
Toward One World:
  The Life of Wendell Willkie
You and Your Shadow
William Howard Taft:
  The President Who Became Chief Justice

IRISH STATESMAN AND REBEL:

The Two Lives of Eamon De Valera

BY BILL SEVERN

BAILEY BROTHERS AND SWINFEN LTD.

FOLKESTONE

IRISH STATESMAN AND REBEL:
The Two Lives of Eamon De Valera

PUBLISHED IN GREAT BRITAIN BY
BAILEY BROS. AND SWINFEN LTD.
FIRST PUBLISHED IN GREAT BRITAIN 1971

COPYRIGHT © 1970 BY Bill Severn

SBN 561-00116-2

PRINTED IN GREAT BRITAIN BY
LATIMER TREND & CO. LTD., WHITSTABLE

❧ ❧

INTRODUCTION

Revolution was the farthest thing from most men's minds in sunny Dublin on the holiday Monday after Easter in 1916. For months, armed groups of citizen volunteers had been parading, marching and holding exercises in public places to dramatize age-old demands for Irish freedom from centuries of British rule. But hardly anybody thought the marching Irish patriots would be "crazy" enough to challenge the military might of the British Empire.

People strolling through the streets and parks, and even British soldiers on holiday leave, stared with little more than passing curiosity at the small bands of the Army of the Irish Republic that marched openly toward strategic sections of the city. They appeared to be staging another routine demonstration. There was no Irish Republic, except in the hearts of men.

But before that day was out the Republic of Ireland would be proclaimed, and for a week the greatly outnumbered and thinly armed rebels would hold Dublin against the overwhelming force of British troops, until the centre of the city was in flaming ruins and the patriots had given the last of their blood and courage to stake their claim of freedom before the world. Their leaders hoped for a miracle of a whole Irish nation that would rise at once to support them, but few expected it to happen, and most of them knew they might die in the attempt. Even their death and defeat, they prayed, would inspire Ireland to revolt.

The Easter Rising began as a tragedy of errors and seemingly ended in failure. Yet it was the beginning of modern Ireland and out of it, in time, rebellion came, and years of bloodshed and strife that led to the slower constitutional growth of a free democratic nation. Ireland became the first nation in the 20th Century to win freedom from foreign domination by its own efforts, and its successful struggle against imperialism foreshadowed revolutionary movements that were to spring up all over a world of dwindling colonial empires, and from the demand of minority groups everywhere for the right to determine their own governments.

Ireland's rise from the ashes of Easter Week in 1916, and its efforts to solve the problems of stability that faced a new nation, were in many ways a preview of what the century was to bring to parts of Asia, Africa and Latin America. It was the first step in the breakaway of the British Empire, the first lesson to the British that they had to give colonial peoples their freedom, and a lesson also to the French and to others who held colonies or domination over far-flung lands. Ireland was the first country in the 20th Century to fight for the belief that no nation should rule another.

Yet Ireland was not a distant colony, but a European nation with deep Christian roots in Western civilization, separated only by the narrow Irish Sea from the British homeland, considered by the British a part of the Kingdom itself. For seven hundred years there had been Irish patriots who rebelled against that conception, and against British rule that sought to wipe out

Ireland's traditional culture and separate identity. By 1916, Ireland's revolutionary leaders were no longer content with Britain's long-delayed promises of better home rule for Ireland. They did not want to be governed better by the British; they wanted the British to get out. But until they made their to-the-death stand at Easter, the Irish rebels were a small minority in a land that had grown complacent.

Most of the leaders of the 1916 Rising were court martialed and shot to death by the British. The only major revolutionist to survive was Eamon De Valera, a man almost unknown to the public before Easter Week when, as the rebel commandant of hardly more than a hundred men, he courageously held out against British fire to delay an army of troop reinforcements from marching on Dublin. Sentenced to death himself, he was imprisoned instead, and upon his release became the leader of Ireland's freedom movement. Many men, including some who later were his bitter enemies, had a part in shaping the new nation, but for well over half a century he was Ireland's dominant political personality, and for much of that time its chosen leader.

A most unlikely rebel, far from a reckless revolutionary, he marched into the Easter Rising as a settled family man of thirty-four, a serious, calm and unemotional professor of mathematics, a scholar with a promising academic career ahead of him, but ready to sacrifice all, even his life if necessary, to lead the full rebellion that came, to raise funds, to put Ireland's position before the world, to hold unswervingly to the ideal of a democratic republic, an Ireland rid of King and Crown.

When the new nation, still to his mind only half-free, was torn by tragic civil war, De Valera found himself on the losing side, no longer able to achieve his ideal of full independence by force. To many he seemed a totally defeated man. But he rose again, no longer as the rebel of arms, but as the elected leader of the people, and worked within the established government to win by constitutional means nearly everything he had sought. Step by constitutional step, he did away with the holds Britain had kept upon Ireland, established its place among the world's independent nations, fathered its new constitution, protected it from a world at war, and led it gradually toward becoming a republic.

The accomplishment was not his alone. Modern Ireland owes its place to no one man. But as prime minister, opposition leader, and president, as the nation's leader for more years than any man led any other 20th Century nation, De Valera was the personification of Ireland's freedom, at home and to the world.

He had two lives: first as a revolutionary, then as a government leader. From the rebel grew the statesman. This is the story, not of modern Ireland's whole history or of all those who shaped it, but of one man who lived twice in the affections of his people.

The author is indebted to many persons in Ireland for their informative conversations, suggestions and help. He particularly would like to thank those in the Department of External Affairs and in the National Library of Ireland for their assistance in making research materials available, and is especially grateful to Mr. Vivion de Valera. The opinions in this book are, of course, the author's and do not necessarily reflect those of anyone else.

❧❧❧❧❧❧❧❧❧❧❧❧❧❧❧❧❧❧❧❧❧❧❧❧❧

CHAPTER 1

De Valera was a native New Yorker, born October 14, 1882, in midtown Manhattan, but was taken back to Ireland while still too young to remember anything of New York, or much about his parents. He grew up in Ireland, his surroundings entirely Irish, and his first real memories were of a country childhood in a small County Limerick farming village, remote in every way from the bustling American big city that was his birthplace.

The Irish in him came from his mother's side of the family. Catherine Coll had left Ireland in 1879 to come to the United States as an immigrant with her brother. A pretty, intelligent girl with a bright personality, she was twenty-one when she arrived in New York. She met and married a Spanish musician, Vivion de Valera, a handsome and well-educated young man several years older than she was, and they made their home not far from St. Agnes' Catholic Church on New York's 43rd Street, where their son was baptized. He was christened Edward and was called "Eddie" by family and friends until as a young man he adopted the Irish version of his name, Eamon.

1

Vivion de Valera earned enough for the family to live on in frugal comfort, but finances became a problem when his health failed. When Eddie was only two years old, his father died. It was impossible for his mother to go out to work and stay home and raise a child. There was no money, no way to keep him and herself, so she made a hard decision.

Her brother, Edmond, who had come to America with her and had been working on a farm in Connecticut, was about to return to Ireland for a visit. He offered to take the boy with him, back to County Limerick, where Eddie's grandmother and another uncle, Patrick Coll, would care for him. In April, 1885, when Eddie was not quite three, Uncle Edmond carried him aboard a ship for the ten-day voyage to Cork, and the train trip some fifty miles north of there to Bruree in the lush green dairy farming land along the River Maigue that was always to be the place he thought of as home.

"The first years of my life that formed my character," he was to say years later, "were lived amongst the Irish people down in Limerick . . . and whenever I wanted to know what the Irish people wanted I had only to examine my own heart."

The Colls lived in a farm labourer's cottage about a mile from the center of the village, a low-roofed rectangular little house with a door that opened directly into the stone-floored kitchen where a fireplace across the far end served for both cooking and heating. There was no running water or indoor plumbing, only smoky paraffin lamps for lighting, and the two rooms that opened off the kitchen made it a somewhat crowded home, especially after Uncle Patrick married and soon added three more children to the household.

But they were a close, happy family, and there was plenty of milk, butter, eggs and plain-cooked food. Grandmother Elizabeth devoted herself to making Eddie feel he belonged and to seeing that he lacked none of the simple things a boy needed.

She became his substitute mother until he was twelve, when she died.

It was from his Irish-speaking grandmother that Eddie learned his first words of the old Gaelic language and heard the tales of Irish folklore. His own beginning English speech soon acquired the slightly harsh County Limerick brogue that always was to sound in his voice. The name De Valera seemed a strange one to his Irish neighbors at first, and he had inherited from his Spanish father the prominent facial features and complexion that gave him a somewhat foreign appearance, but the villagers quickly accepted him as being as Irish as the rest of the Colls.

He was five when he was sent with the other children of his parish district to the square gray stone schoolhouse that stood behind a wall in a cobbled yard at the far end of the village. His first schoolmaster, John Kelly, an elderly gentleman, was a painstaking teacher who constantly stressed the values of a good education and the virtues of a Christian life. He told the boys that hard learning was the way to get the things they wanted most, and once said to Eddie that if he persevered at his studies someday he would have "a bicycle and a good watch and chain."

Eddie was not precocious, but intelligent, persistent, and hungry for the knowledge that offered such rewards. He quickly learned to read, showed an early aptitude for mathematics, and as he grew a little older became skilled in language and composition. Soon he was at the head of his class and schoolmaster Kelly asked him to help tutor some of the other boys.

Farm chores were part of his daily life before and after school. He learned to harness the horse and donkey, tended goats, milked the cows, cleaned out the cowhouse, followed the tumbler rake, took his place on top of the rick, and forked loads of hay. For sport, he ran foot races and played the Irish games of hurling and Gaelic football. When there was no other way to use up his athletic energy, he went hiking, exploring the ruins of an ancient castle in the hills, or searching the fields for hidden springs.

By the time he was fourteen, at an age when most Bruree boys finished schooling and began their life's work on the farms, he had become such an exceptional student that both his schoolmaster and his priest urged his uncle to let him gain additional education. Although it would mean expense the family was hard-pressed to afford, Uncle Patrick agreed to send him as a day student to what amounted to a high school, run by the Christian Brothers in Charleville. It was only about six miles away, and he could take an early train there in the mornings and walk back in the afternoons.

He studied so hard that neighbors began to say his face was always buried in a book. Sometimes they would see him seated along the roadside, scanning pages as if he couldn't wait to get home to read. At the supper table there would be a book propped beside him, and when he drove the milk cart to the village creamery he would sit reading while he waited his turn in line. On his own he read every borrowed book he could lay his hands upon, especially those that told of the exciting adventures of the old Irish heroes.

More directly, he learned from the monks at school, and from Bruree's own story-tellers, about Ireland's history of battles, rebellions, famine and economic suffering, of the centuries of oppression by British rulers and land-owners, and of the crushing of Ireland's culture and language, but never its spirit to be free. When Uncle Patrick's neighbors gathered in the farm kitchen in the evenings to talk, and often to debate Ireland's current quarrels with Britain, he learned something, too, of politics.

But for the most part, as his uncle later recalled, politics didn't much interest Eddie as a boy. When the kitchen talk turned political, he was apt to move off to the fireplace corner and pick up another book to study. He knew he would have to make his own way in life and he was determined to succeed. His mother's letters from America had brought the news that she had remarried and settled in Rochester, New York, on an estate where her new husband, Charles Wheelwright, groomed horses and was a carriage driver.

Suddenly, at sixteen, Eddie found himself lifted out of Bruree and into Ireland's great city of Dublin. At the school in Charleville he had won academic awards during each of his two years of study and the Christian Brothers were so pleased they recommended him for a college scholarship. In the fall of 1898 he left his Bruree home to enter Blackrock College, just a few miles outside central Dublin, in the suburbs overlooking the Bay.

At Blackrock he came into his own as an athlete and scholar. Toweringly tall, long-legged, slim but powerfully built, he had a striking physical appearance: intense brown eyes, bold nose, firm mouth, and a purposeful stride, shoulders back and head erect. His popularity with his classmates was partly because he was a star of the football team and a champion runner in track meets, but the Catholic fathers who ran the school were more impressed with his scholastic record and strength of character.

He was still a student at Blackrock when he began his own teaching career. The college appointed him as a junior instructor in mathematics for intermediate classes and before he was twenty he was promoted to instruct senior classes. While he was reading for his own college courses and achieving honors in them, he was conducting classes at Blackrock several hours each day. He prepared for his university degree at Dublin's old Royal University, and at the age of twenty-two, in 1904, became a graduate in mathematical science, and started the full-time teaching that he expected would be his life's profession.

His superiors at Blackrock chose him to fill a staff vacancy at Rockwell College, not far from Cashel in Tipperary County, and De Valera became Rockwell's new Professor of Mathematics and Physics. He taught there for a year, pedaling his bicycle into Cashel and hiking in the hills for outdoor exercise. In Rockwell's classrooms he was in charge of honor students, some of whom won awards and competitions.

But Dublin offered more opportunity and he returned to take post-graduate courses there himself while he taught at various schools and colleges in and around the city. Students remembered him as an excellent teacher, patient and able to relate class work to their everyday experiences, but one who demanded hard study, constant drilling in fundamentals, and precise answers. Mathematics, his chosen subject, was mostly what he taught, but he also instructed classes in French and Latin. After teaching groups that ranged from boarding school boys and convent girls to medical students and young men preparing for the priesthood, he settled into the steady position of Professor of Mathematics at Carysfort Training College for young women who expected to become primary school teachers.

All through his college years he had managed to get back to Bruree during the summers, to pitch in and help with the farm work, and to go hunting game birds, a sport at which he had become a crack shot. But another interest began to draw him to Bruree, the chance to talk to villagers, those who could speak Irish. He had been relearning the language, remembering its sounds and phrases from childhood, and there was no better place to test his new learning than in conversation with the old men of Bruree.

Like many young Dubliners close to the universities he had been inspired by the revival of native culture that was sweeping Ireland, by the rebirth of national spirit in plays and poetry, and in newly emerging political movements. If most of Ireland's older generation complacently still looked to London for better government, many younger men and women were listening to the new voices that called upon the Irish to look to their own traditional strength to change things.

De Valera's interest at first was intellectual, not political, but when he joined the Gaelic League in 1908 he took a long step into a different life. Founded some years before by Professor Douglas Hyde, a poet and scholar, and dedicated to the ideal of uniting Irishmen of all religious and political beliefs in a common cause of cultural nationalism, the League was devoted to reviving the national language and traditions. Whatever changes came in government, its followers argued, would bring no real freedom as long as Irishmen remained British in culture and values. Ireland had to be rid of alien English influence. "In our language lies our great hope," De Valera was to say. "Our language is our character."

For young Ireland the Gaelic League was a way of life as well as a cause. Members of hundreds of branches that flourished across the country shared in the learning of Irish, reading Irish literature, playing Irish music, singing Irish songs, dancing Irish dances, spending holidays in Irish-speaking districts, and absorbing everything that was Irish. For De Valera, among other things, it meant changing his name from Edward to the Irish form of Eamon, and as an educator, pursuing a greater knowledge of the language.

He enrolled in the Leinster College of Irish where his teacher was not only an ardent Gaelic Leaguer but also a very attractive young woman, and his pursuit soon became as romantic as it was intellectual. He was not alone in his feelings. Half the young men in her class trailed along to walk her home in the evenings when the lessons ended, not that she encouraged any one more than the others, until De Valera came along.

She also had changed her name, from Janie O'Flanagan to

the Irish that she always preferred, Sinead ni Fhlannagain. Five years older than he was, born in Eastern Ireland, where her family were tradespeople, she was brought up in a home where nationalist feelings were strong. But like De Valera she was not a native speaker of Irish. She had learned enough to be a good teacher and they were to go on learning together, teaching each other, promoting the national language all their lives. When he had become world-famous, Sinead would establish her own fame as a writer of Irish folk tales for children.

When they met she was better known than he was, as a petite golden-haired amateur actress who had played leading roles in some of the first Gaelic plays ever produced in Dublin. Among those who came to her Irish classes at Leinster College was the future playwright, Sean O'Casey. But Sinead was more impressed with young Professor De Valera, as he was with her. The Gaelic League, as well as their personal feelings, drew them together. Sharing its songs and dances, meetings and holiday excursions, they fell in love, and in January, 1910, they were married.

He was twenty-eight when they moved into the two-storey brick terrace house in a narrow street of suburban Donnybrook that was to be their home. There, as the year 1910 ended, their first son was born, a boy they named Vivion for the father De Valera had hardly known.

Established in the teaching profession, spoken of as a "born teacher," with the promise of a rewarding career, De Valera wanted nothing more than to settle down to the happiness of family life, except for one thing: an Irish nation. That, he wanted more, and the first step he had taken into the Gaelic League already was leading him to others, far more dangerous, in the cause of Irish independence.

❧ ❧

CHAPTER 2

Eamon De Valera took up a gun for Ireland with deliberate decision. He was not an impulsive man and he weighed his responsibilities. His family had grown with the birth of a daughter, Mairin, soon to be followed by two more sons, Eamonn and Brian. Because of the need for more money at home he again was teaching extra classes in addition to his full-time professorship at Carysfort. He had little time for anything but his family and his work and almost his only outside activity was the Gaelic League.

But the League had become a fountainhead of change for Ireland. At its meetings De Valera drank deeply of the new nationalism flowing into other movements. For those more interested in sports than in language there was the Gaelic Athletic Association, which encouraged traditional Irish games and discouraged those considered alien English. There were women's organizations, and an Irish scouting group that filled young minds with the glory of Ireland's old heroes and sought to train boys "to fight Ireland's battle when they are men."

Politically the still small but growing Sinn Fein group was

9

attracting men like De Valera. Its Gaelic name, roughly trans-
lated, meant "Ourselves Alone," and it called upon the Irish to
develop their native resources, self-reliance and independence,
to look to themselves and not to anything the British Parliament
might do. Founded and led by journalist Arthur Griffith, who
believed England had "one hand on Ireland's throat and the
other in her pocket," Sinn Fein urged passive, bloodless
resistance, not revolution, in the beginning. Griffith wanted
Ireland's members of the British Parliament to leave it and to
help set up an Irish government in Dublin. He advocated a dual
monarchy with England, like that of Austria-Hungary.

Working in secret behind all the Irish movements and
organizations, infiltrating them, influencing them, gaining control of key positions and carefully recruiting men who could be
counted upon to follow its orders when the time came, was the
underground Irish Republican Brotherhood. Bound by oath to
strict secrecy, and never operating in the open, its members
plotted complete separation from England, independence and
a free Republic of Ireland.

Founded a half-century before, with some of its beginnings
in America and with most of its funds supplied by closely allied
Irish-Americans, it had been revived by new and active leaders,
dedicated revolutionists who were gathering the strength to
strike. De Valera's ardent patriotism had been noticed by such
men. Although he was reluctant to be part of any secret
organization, he soon was drawn into the Irish Republican
Brotherhood.

But Ireland's first open threat of armed rebellion came from
men with a far different purpose, the Ulstermen of the North
who were determined not to set the country free but to keep it
entirely British. Descendants of settlers who had been sent there
generations before by Protestant England to colonize, dominate
and take over Catholic Ireland, they had risen to power and

prestige in the area around Belfast, where they were the ruling majority. Tied to England by industrial and financial interests as well as by Protestant tradition and pride in Empire, they believed that Ireland's prosperity, and their own, depended upon preserving its firm union with England. They feared being part of any government controlled by the rest of Catholic Ireland, in which they would become a minority.

In Britain's Parliament, after years of frustration, Ireland's representatives, the Irish Nationalist Party headed by John Redmond, finally had brought Home Rule for Ireland close to reality. The British Liberals, who held power in Parliament with Irish Party support, were moving to give Ireland limited self-government. The Irish were to have their own parliament in Dublin, but Ireland still would be ruled by the King, by British forces and officials, with no voice in the affairs of nations, and with strict British controls over trade, finances, taxes, schools and laws.

For De Valera and men like him, it was far from enough, but to most of the Irish people the promise of Home Rule seemed better than nothing, and the great majority backed Redmond's efforts for constitutional change. Up North in the area around Belfast, however, that possibility outraged the Ulster Unionists and they rose to fight any attempt by the British Parliament to force it upon them.

Two hundred thousand Ulstermen took solemn oaths, some of them written with their blood, to resist Irish Home Rule. Led by famed lawyer Edward Carson, who was the uncompromising voice of the Unionists in Parliament, and organized by veteran Captain James Craig, they began forming their own army. By their show of force, they intended to thwart the British Parliament, even if that meant setting up a provisional government to separate the counties of Ulster from the rest of Ireland.

The Ulstermen had strong and open support in England from the British Conservative Party, whose leader, Bonar Law, came to Belfast in person to encourage them to fight Home Rule to the limit of their resistance. High British Army officers also gave the Ulstermen support and advice and British officials refused to interfere as Carson's volunteer army staged bristling military demonstrations. But the armed threat from Ireland's North brought swift answer from the South. In Dublin, the men who wanted Ireland's freedom also armed themselves.

De Valera, in November, 1913, became among the first to enroll in the Irish Volunteers, organized as a citizens' army "to secure and maintain the rights and liberties common to all the people of Ireland" by "defensive and protective" means. Its men were "to drill, to learn the use of arms, to acquire the habit of concerted and disciplined action" so as to "renew the vitality of the nation . . . and bring back to every town, village and countryside . . . the sense of free men who have fitted themselves to defend the cause of freedom."

The Irish Republican Brotherhood had a strong but secret hand in forming the Volunteers. There was no way they could openly arm and train men for a Republican uprising against the British. Such a revolutionary force, if its true purpose were known, would have been quickly suppressed. But the Gaelic League's vice-president, Eoin MacNeill, an eminent historian and professor of Ancient Irish at Dublin's University College, had suggested launching a Volunteer movement to answer the challenge to Home Rule, and the I.R.B. seized the opportunity.

MacNeill became chairman of the Irish Volunteers, with the Brotherhood's full motives kept from him, and others of various political views were brought into its leadership. Large numbers of those who joined the Volunteers wanted no complete separation from the British Empire, certainly not by force. They were supporters of Redmond and Home Rule. Many signed up without clear political reasons of any kind, simply as Irishmen, joyful that at last the Irish were to have their own army.

De Valera entered the ranks as one among four thousand Irish Volunteers, with no special uniform at first, dressed as most of them were in ordinary work clothes, to which he added a deerstalker's cap. But he stood out as a singularly impressive figure, well over six feet tall, with somber burning eyes and a harsh strong voice. He was described by one of his friends of those days as "laughter-loving, glad and pensive, sad and happy all combined."

Eight public halls were rented for drilling the men in Dublin and fifteen companies of Volunteers were formed in the city as others began to organize throughout Ireland. They had no knowledge of soldiering, no military manuals, little equipment. Lacking guns many drilled by shouldering wooden staves. They were working men whose time free from everyday occupations was limited. For De Valera, burdened with a heavy teaching schedule, training with the Volunteers meant sacrificing time at home with his family, but Sinead strongly shared his views and managed the household and the children so that he had few domestic problems.

By the end of the year the Volunteers were ten thousand strong and they eventually grew to a force of 180,000. Young men trained in the Irish scouting clubs and others who had served in the British Army became drill instructors. Women formed auxiliary units to study signaling and first aid. Dublin Volunteer companies, each of one hundred men, were grouped according to the locality of their homes and democratically elected their own officers. De Valera's company soon chose him their captain.

Meanwhile another army of citizens had come out of Dublin's wretched slums and the homes of its underpaid labouring men to march in its streets. In the beginning they had no connection with the Irish Volunteers. Labour troubles had brought weeks of violence and suffering that started when police charged into a mass meeting near Liberty Hall, headquarters of the Irish Transport and General Workers Union, and clubbed supporters of a tramway strike, leaving scores injured and three dead. Four hundred Dublin employers banded together to break the union, refusing to employ its members, and there were more strikes, lockouts, arrests and police attacks. Thousands of workers were unemployed and one-third of the city was near starvation.

Union leaders called upon the workers to form a citizens' army in their own defense, and James Connolly, a union organizer, Irish nationalist and socialist founder of the Irish Labour Party, soon took charge of drilling armed union members in military formation. Connolly, a self-educated man who was forced to go to work himself at the age of eleven, had printed and edited the first Irish socialist newspaper and had spent seven years in America as a pioneer organizer for the Industrial Workers of the World before returning to Ireland.

"The cause of labour is the cause of Ireland," Connolly preached, "and the cause of Ireland is the cause of labour." The great Dublin strike failed, but the union's citizen army remained, and under Connolly's energetic leadership became a well-trained fighting force, dedicated to his ideal of an independent socialist Irish Republic.

Faced with rising forces of violence, the British issued a proclamation prohibiting the importing of arms into Ireland, which was ignored in both the North and South. In April, 1914, the Ulstermen succeeded in bringing ashore thirty-five thousand rifles and other munitions bought in Germany, while British officials looked the other way and made no attempt to stop them. Meanwhile all over Europe nations were mobilizing for a far greater violence, the First World War.

Captain De Valera's first confrontation with British soldiers came on a Sunday in late July, 1914. His company of Irish Volunteers, like the rest, were still almost unarmed. As on any Sunday they started out on what appeared to Dublin's police to be a routine morning parade, which aroused no unusual suspicion. Well-kept, even from most of the Volunteers themselves, was the secret that for months a group of sympathizers had been raising funds in London and organizing plans to match the Ulstermen in gun-running from Germany.

Erskine Childers, who master-minded the plot, was the son of a prominent English father and an Irish mother, a Cambridge honors graduate, British veteran of the Boer War, and until not long before had been a committee clerk in London's House of Commons. Childers bought fifteen hundred secondhand guns in Hamburg, smuggled them through Belgium, and had them put aboard a tugboat, which he met with his own small yacht, the *Asgard*, in the North Sea. Evading British patrols, he sailed the yacht, with his wife among the crew, right up to the quay at Howth, northeast of Dublin, to which the Volunteers had marched that July Sunday.

When the men realized that at last they were to get guns they were so eager to rip open the crates and arm themselves that some almost pushed others into the water. Within twenty minutes one thousand Irish Volunteers had guns to shoulder and other weapons had been hurried off by motor car to pre-arranged hiding places. The operation was deliberately carried out in broad daylight to arouse public enthusiasm and pride in the Volunteer army.

With their new guns, the elated men marched back toward Dublin, and as word went ahead of them people lined the roads to cheer. Telegraph wires had been cut in an attempt to keep authorities at Dublin Castle, the center of British administration in Ireland, from being alerted, but the news reached the British despite the cut wires and city police, supported by a detachment of the King's Own Scottish Borderers, marched out to halt the Volunteers and seize their guns.

De Valera's men and the other Volunteers were halted at Contarf by a roadblock and a phalanx of soldiers with fixed bayonets. There was brief scuffling and the British grabbed some guns and broke them. While officers up front argued with the British, the rest of the Volunteers scattered and escaped. The British managed to capture only nineteen guns and the main body of Volunteers saved their weapons by running off with them to places where they could be hidden until later.

There was indignation in Dublin when people heard that British troops had been turned against the Volunteers while up in Belfast the Ulstermen were allowed to parade their arms with no interference. As the frustrated British soldiers returned from Clontarf through Dublin's Bachelor's Walk, a crowd hooted and stoned them. Angered and frightened, the British opened fire upon the sidewalk crowd. They shot and wounded thirty-two unarmed people and killed a woman and two men.

To shocked and enraged Dubliners it brought home the sense of being a people whose country was occupied by alien force. British authorities held an inquiry but found the soldiers blameless and whitewashed the affair. Nothing could have done more to rally the people to the support of the Volunteers. There was a great public funeral for the victims of the shooting, in which the coffins were followed by Volunteers in military formation, and salutes were fired over the graves.

One week later Ireland was engulfed in the First World War. The British Parliament declared war against Germany and its allies, and Ireland, because of union with Britain, was forced to fight on the side of what some Irishmen considered their only real enemy, the British. Sinn Fein's Arthur Griffith wrote: "Ireland is not at war with Germany. She is not at war with any continental power . . . the only duty we can have is to stand for Ireland's interests, irrespective of the interests of England or Germany or any other foreign country."

The war divided the passions of the Irish. Great numbers who favored Home Rule but no break with the Empire answered Britain's call for help. A quarter of a million Irishmen were recruited into the British armed forces. British Prime Minister Herbert Asquith spoke of "fighting to vindicate the principle that small nationalities are not to be crushed . . . by the arbitrary will of a stronger and overmastering power," and many Irish believed that was England's pledge to see justice done in Ireland when the war was won.

Followers of Ireland's leader in Parliament, John Redmond, considered Home Rule all but achieved. But while a Home Rule Act finally had been put on the British statute books it was nullified by another act that postponed putting it into effect during the war, and meanwhile amendments that threatened the partition of Ulster from the rest of Ireland hung over it. When Redmond himself called upon the Irish to join the British armed forces, it was a call that shattered the ranks of the Irish Volunteers. The great majority, some 170,000 Volunteers, finally voted to support Redmond. Only a small core of about 15,000 Volunteers were left who believed Ireland's cause had to be put before England's.

De Valera was among them. Home Rule, to the ardent nationalists, had finally failed. The suspended law seemed to them a farce, a complete nullity, more a threat to Ireland's future than a promise. He cast his lot with those who saw armed revolt against the British as the only way to awaken the people to demand true freedom, by bringing alive a Republic of Ireland. Even if it were quickly crushed, they would give it root and reality, and a sacrifice of blood to nourish it in Irish hearts.

CHAPTER 3

Eamon De Valera was moved up into a command position as the Irish Volunteers became a secret army within an army under control of the Irish Republican Brotherhood. He had no part in the high councils of the Brotherhood, but he was close to men who had and he was taken into its confidence as an officer who would be prepared to follow its orders when the time came for armed uprising against the British.

He was made Adjutant Commander of the Dublin Brigade, directly under the command of his friend Thomas MacDonagh, one of the men at the top of the secret Brotherhood, and one of seven who were to sign the proclamation of the Irish Republic. De Valera and MacDonagh, a poet, critic and university teacher of literature, had become acquainted through the Gaelic League and were intimate comrades in the Volunteers.

Another whom De Valera had first known in Gaelic League activities was Patrick Henry Pearse, who had been editor of the League's magazine and a dominant figure in the Gaelic revival movement. A lawyer turned educator, founder and headmaster of schools that pioneered in teaching Irish, Pearse had become

19

a leading voice of nationalism as an essayist, poet, playwright and forceful orator. His courage and his visionary faith in the Republic were to provide a heritage of inspiration for the Irish people. As the secret link between the command of the Volunteers and that of the Irish Republican Brotherhood, Pearse was the mainspring of the insurrection he helped plot and lead.

The official Chief of Staff of the Volunteers, Eoin MacNeill, and other officers known to be opposed to the use of arms except for defensive resistance, were told nothing of the Brotherhood's plans for immediate rebellion against the British. Officially Pearse was only MacNeill's organization chief, but in that position he signed MacNeill's orders to the men, and the rank and file were used to seeing Pearse's name on them. When the time came for the Rising, Pearse would sign orders again, but they would be his own.

De Valera knew, as few others did, that at any moment he might be called upon to lead his men into battle against the greatest Empire in the world. He waited and watched rebellion grow. The Volunteers filled the countryside every weekend with marchers who carried guns, staged mock attacks against Dublin's public buildings, and warned the British that any attempt to take their weapons from them would be resisted with force. Members of the women's auxiliary paraded in uniform, banners of rebellion were flown, and writers and speakers openly called for revolution. But hardly anybody realized that definite plans for it were in the making.

Arthur Griffith's Sinn Fein was broadening into a political party identified by the public with the Volunteers and with all shades of extreme national opposition to the British. Almost anyone actively against Home Rule and the recruiting of Irishmen into the British armed forces was regarded as a "Sinn Feiner." But Griffith himself, although an ardent nationalist, was given no hand in the revolutionary plans the Brotherhood was making with utmost secrecy. Its leaders in Ireland and its friends in organizations in America had become determined not to let the First World War end, whether England or Germany eventually won, without creating an Irish Republic.

De Valera already was being watched by the British, if only because he was seen in the company of MacDonagh and others who were being followed by detectives from Dublin Castle. He went on teaching his classes, meeting socially with friends, being with his wife and children, giving no hint of what was to come.

The British were aware of much that was going on, but were confident they could crush any real insurrection. Anxious not to inflame Irish feeling against them even more, they also were wary of doing anything that might offend American or world opinion. They made some arrests, which only increased Irish resistance to their recruiting campaigns; they raided and shut down some nationalist newspapers, which quickly began publishing again under other names from other printing plants.

Meanwhile labour leader John Connolly was becoming so impatient for revolution that the Irish Republican Brotherhood feared he and his army of union men might prematurely start one on their own. Word reached the Brotherhood that Connolly was about to march, so I.R.B. agents kidnapped him and held him for three days in Dublin while they talked things over with him. The Brotherhood took him into their confidence, explained their plans, and the result was that Connolly agreed to cooperate and combine his army with the Volunteers. "From the moment the first shot is fired," Connolly said, "there will no longer be Volunteers or Citizen Army, but only the Army of the Irish Republic."

Early in January, 1916, the preliminary plans were put into operation. The Brotherhood's military council first set Easter Sunday, April 23, as the date for the Rising. Friends in America were alerted and a message was sent through them to Berlin by way of the German embassy in Washington. Germany, anxious to encourage rebellion in Ireland against the British, previously had promised help. An answer came back that the Germans would deliver a shipload of 20,000 rifles, some machine guns, explosives, and one million rounds of ammunition to Tralee Bay on the Atlantic coast of Ireland between April 20 and 22, which would be from Thursday to Saturday of the week before Easter.

But everything went wrong that could go wrong. After the trawler *Aud* had set out from Germany with the vital weapons, the revolutionary council in Dublin, not knowing that it had already sailed, changed plans. The Irish leaders decided that the Monday after Easter, instead of Easter Sunday, would be a better day for revolution. It would be a Bank Holiday when most of the British officers and men would be off duty and many would be out of the city attending annual horse races at the Fairyhouse race course twenty miles from Dublin.

Another message was sent to the Germans by way of America not to bring the munitions to Tralee Bay until Easter Sunday night, just before the uprising, because the guns could not be smuggled ashore days in advance without alerting the British. Warning came back that it was too late to change plans. The *Aud*, running through British wartime patrols in secrecy, had no wireless aboard, so it was impossible to set a new time for its arrival. But the warning never reached the revolutionaries in Dublin. It was intercepted and decoded by the British Admiralty.

The Irish leaders went ahead with their new plans for a revolution on Easter Monday, not knowing that the guns they needed would arrive days too early, when nobody would be there to meet the *Aud* except British warships. Confident that everything had been arranged, they also did not know that their secret agent in Germany, Sir Roger Casement, was trying to race to Ireland aboard a German submarine to warn them to call off their plans. Casement, previously knighted by England for distinguished work in the British Consular Service, but Irish-born and long an active worker in the Irish cause, had been bitterly disappointed by Germany's failure to send more help for the rebellion, including battle-trained German officers.

De Valera got his secret orders from MacDonagh and the revolutionary Brotherhood as Easter approached, but the secret remained well-kept from Volunteer Chief of Staff MacNeill and other Volunteer officers who might oppose the rebellion if they knew. The men in the ranks of the Volunteers were not informed that anything but routine maneuvers were planned. A public announcement had been made that three days of maneuvers would be held over Easter weekend.

Three thousand Volunteers were expected to report to the four battalions of the Dublin Brigade, to be ordered on Monday after Easter to seize and fortify strategic points in the city. Combined troops under the personal command of James Connolly were to capture the General Post Office so the Provisional Government of the Republic could establish headquarters there. De Valera would command the Third Battalion to block the rail lines and main road into Dublin from Kingstown (Dun Laoghaire) harbour, to halt any British troop reinforcements landed from England. Such were the plans.

Throughout all of Ireland men were expected to rise in arms at the same time in every city and village, to take control of bridges, roads and buildings, overpower British officials and the constabulary, and after each area was secure to send reinforcements marching into Dublin from the countryside. There were 13,000 Volunteers in the provinces outside Dublin, spread out in small bands of guerilla fighters, with revolutionary commanders ready to take charge and give orders for the long-planned operations.

But the men in the provinces had few guns or explosives.

Successful rebellion would depend almost entirely on the weapons expected from Germany. The Republican leaders, unaware that the *Aud* had never received its changed instructions, took it for granted that the ship would reach Tralee Bay late on Easter evening, so its cargo could be quickly distributed and run over dark roads during the early morning hours to men waiting in Cork, Tipperary, Limerick and the West.

As the week before Easter began, the secret seven-member military council met, constituted themselves a provisional government, and drew up the Proclamation of the Irish Republic, which was written mostly by Pearse, who was chosen first President of the Republic. De Valera quit his professorship at Carysfort Training College and walked out of the classroom to which he would never return. For the rest of the week, his full time was taken with planning the operations of his own battalion and as Adjutant Commander of the entire Dublin Brigade. There were orders, messages, detailed assignments.

Such active military preparations in Dublin and all over Ireland made it obvious to many of the Volunteers that something more than routine maneuvers was planned. Rumors grew and spread and were carried to Chief of Staff MacNeill. He finally called Pearse into his office on Thursday and demanded the truth. Pearse admitted plans for the Rising were underway. MacNeill answered that he intended to prevent it by every means short of betraying its leaders to the British. He moved immediately to regain full control of the Volunteers and to countermand all orders except his own.

That same Thursday afternoon the Germans evaded British patrols and brought the *Aud* alongside Inishtooskert Island in Tralee Bay, but no pilot boat came out to meet them and there were no signs of activity on the lonely shore. The Irish, following their own schedule, did not expect the *Aud* to come until three days later. The German captain waited through the night for signal lights from shore and by then was spotted by British warships. The *Aud* was surrounded, a shot was fired across its bow, and it was ordered into Queenstown harbor. The German officers and crew tried to escape and were captured, but not before they managed to blow up and sink the *Aud* and its cargo of munitions.

Roger Casement meanwhile had arrived by German submarine in Tralee Bay, where he put off for shore in a rowboat with two companions. He was caught and arrested by the British, who alerted authorities in Dublin Castle, and tight restrictions were imposed so no word about the German submarine or the blowing up of the *Aud* would leak out. The British apparently were convinced that any plans for an Easter insurrection had been wrecked and that there would now be no uprising. Without hurry, they considered how to deal with the revolutionary leaders to their best advantage, since the German arms ship and submarine could be used to sway public opinion as proof of treasonable connections with Britain's enemy at war.

As far as the Irish leaders in Dublin yet knew, the *Aud* was still on its way toward a Sunday night arrival. De Valera, concerned over the growing danger that the British might try to seize and imprison known revolutionaries, slept at home Thursday night without taking off his uniform, a revolver close to his bedside. It would be a long time before he slept at home again.

Friday morning Pearse and MacDonagh had another conference with MacNeill and revealed to him for the first time that a shipload of arms was on its way from Germany. They managed to persuade MacNeill that plans had gone too far to be halted. MacNeill reluctantly agreed to rescind his orders and let them go ahead and that afternoon the revolutionary military council secretly took possession of the Volunteers' building

and began issuing commands for revolution once more. But
the next day a messenger finally reached them in Dublin and
they knew the truth about what had happened in Tralee.

Pearse argued with MacNeill that they had to carry out the
revolution without delay or the British would make sweeping
arrests of the Volunteers. MacNeill, however, decided there no
longer was any hope of success and that in the circumstances
it would be suicidal for young, unprepared Volunteers to go
into action. He called off all plans, sent messages throughout
the country definitely countermanding insurrection, and made
public announcements.

MacNeill even went so far as to put an advertisement in
what was then Dublin's largest Sunday newspaper, the *Sunday
Independent*, giving notice that "owing to the very critical position, all orders given to Irish Volunteers for tomorrow, Easter
Sunday, are hereby rescinded, and no parades, marches, or
other movements of Irish Volunteers will take place" and that
each individual Volunteer was to "obey this order strictly in
every particular." He sent a personal order on Sunday to
De Valera: "As Chief of Staff, I have ordered and hereby
order that no movement whatsoever of Irish Volunteers is to
be made today. You will carry out this order in your own
command and make it known to other commands."

The British were even more relieved when they read the
newspaper advertisement calling off a revolution. It now
seemed definite that there would be no Easter "disorders." In
every part of Ireland, Volunteers received the news with dis-
may. They had been confused by rumors, conflicting commands, and now there was the firm cancellation of all plans.
Any hope of nationwide rebellion, foredoomed to failure any-
how without the weapons from the *Aud*, was at an end.

Easter Sunday morning the revolutionary leaders met at
Dublin's Liberty Hall. Despite the despair of some, they decided

that revolution, in Dublin at least, should go on. Democratically, they took a vote, and voted in favor of rebellion on Monday at noon. It was also a vote to die in what now could be only a protest, but with faith that the spirit of the Republic would live.

MacDonagh sent out a Sunday order to the Dublin Brigade. All Volunteers were to remain in Dublin. It said no more than that, but for the men who knew, it was an alert for revolution. Beneath MacDonagh's name, De Valera signed his own. He then went home to spend a few last hours with his wife and children. On Monday morning another order went out, for the Dublin battalions to "parade for inspection and route march."

Half the Volunteers, not knowing what orders to obey, failed to report. Even with Connolly's citizen army of union men added, there were only some twelve hundred to stand against the British, and twice that many were needed to hold the strongpoints in Dublin as planned. Connolly was asked, "Is there no hope?" He answered, "None whatever. We are going out to be slaughtered." De Valera said nothing. He exchanged salutes and went out to lead his dwindled battalion.

CHAPTER 4

Commandant Eamon De Valera marched his 130 green-uniformed soldiers through the sunny streets of Dublin at high noon the Monday after Easter, almost ignored by strolling citizens out to enjoy the holiday. The people were long-accustomed to the sight of marching groups and the open display of old guns and revolvers caused no excitement.

Without opposition, and within an hour or so, other units of the Army of the Republic had occupied the strongpoints and were spreading thin forces to fortify supporting positions. Telegraph lines were cut, but telephone communications were neglected, so that when the British realized the rebellion was real they were able to send quick calls for troops from areas surrounding Dublin. The rebels provided themselves with no communication except by foot messenger, which soon became almost impossible.

Lack of manpower kept them from seizing Dublin Castle, or Trinity College which was to become a British artillery base. Militarily the General Post Office, hemmed in by other buildings at the downtown heart of the city, was a poor choice for headquarters, but it was the most central public place, and there the poets and scholars commanding the rebellion dug in for grim, defensive battle.

They ran up the tricolor flag that was to symbolize the hope of one united nation, the white of peace in the center bringing together the Orange and the Green. Gaels and Scotch-English, Irish Catholics and Irish Protestants, were promised by the flag itself an Ireland without partition, for all its people. From the Post Office steps, Pearse read the beautifully-worded and moving Proclamation of the Irish Republic:

"In the name of God and of the dead generations from which she receives her old tradition of nationhood, Ireland, through us, summons her children to her flag and strikes for her freedom. . . .

"We declare the right of the people of Ireland to the ownership of Ireland, and to the unfettered control of Irish destinies, to be sovereign and indefeasible. The long usurpation of that right by a foreign people and government has not extinguished the right, nor can it ever be extinguished except by the destruction of the Irish people. . . . Standing on that fundamental right and again asserting it in arms in the face of the world, we hereby proclaim the Irish Republic as a Sovereign Independent State, and we pledge our lives and the lives of our comrades-in-arms to the cause of its freedom, of its welfare, and of its exaltation among the nations. . . .

"The Republic guarantees religious and civil liberty, equal rights and equal opportunities to all its citizens, and declares its resolve to pursue the happiness and prosperity of the whole nation and of all its parts, cherishing all the children of the nation equally, and oblivious of the differences carefully fostered by an alien government, which have divided a minority from the majority in the past . . ."

Most of the small crowd that had gathered to hear Pearse,

Commanding General and first President of the Provisional Government of the Irish Republic, were astonished. Some were indignant, some laughed and turned away; others listened with amazement, unable to believe that these "political cranks" really hoped to start a revolution.

Far more astonished were the railroad passengers at Westland Row Station, the terminus of the rail line from Kingstown to Dublin, when a dozen soldiers sent by De Valera rushed through to the platform, seized control of the station and spread out along the tracks, ready to shoot if they met resistance. But, as elsewhere in the city, there was as yet no opposition.

De Valera meanwhile led the main force of his battalion to Boland's bakery and mill, Dublin's largest bread making plant, and took over its big slant-roofed buildings as his area headquarters. Boland's was in a strategic position commanding land, water and rail approaches to the central city. Spreading his men carefully, two in one place, three in another, to hold a very large perimeter and a complex of buildings, De Valera extended token detachments to give an impression of strength along streets, bridges and a canal, to the railroad and the riverfront. His men were positioned where their constant sniping would contain the British forces in nearby Beggars' Bush barracks.

He decided that if the British landed reinforcements from England at Kingstown their main line of march would bring them along Northumberland Road, across the Mount Street Bridge, which would bear the brunt of the attack. Two men were placed in a big stone house at the corner of Northumberland Road, a long block away from the bridge. Other homes along both sides of the street, and a parochial hall, were taken over and put in a state of defense. A section commander, George Reynolds, and six Volunteers occupied Clanwilliam House, just across the bridge and facing it. De Valera sent home some very young Volunteers, realizing few of the men in the outposts would survive when the full attack came.

A small crowd, mostly youngsters from the surrounding slum area of the old section of Dublin, had gathered in front of Boland's to see what was happening, and they also were sent home, with a warning to stay under cover. Guards were stationed in every section of the bakery and De Valera told the day workers to go home and take with them whatever bread they required. But dough mixtures had been prepared for the night shift of bakers, and he agreed that it shouldn't be wasted; it was needed by the people of Dublin, as well as to feed his own men. So the production of bread went on almost as usual for a time. Soldiers barricaded the main gate of Boland's with flour bags, but some of the staff was passed in through a rear entrance and those who came in were not allowed out again.

The mill room was dark, oppressively hot, filled with the odors of dough from a fermentation loft directly above that formed a low ceiling, so that De Valera had to duck his head as he moved about. On the ground floor, where the huge bread ovens were moved out on iron tracks, he ordered his men to sandbag the walls with more bags of flour. They ate some of the bread, and for warmth slept between the walls and the ovens. Other men, stationed at the high windows in the bakery and in a granary, broke out the glass to clear the openings for firing their guns.

Sharp firing was underway at other Republican positions closer to downtown Dublin by Monday night and there was a brief action at one of De Valera's outposts. His snipers attacked a body of veteran British guards marching toward Beggars' Bush barracks, killing five and wounding seven. He was incessantly on the move, going from floor to floor of the bakery, out into the cobbled yards and along the lines of defense, checking sentry posts, giving orders. When he found one post deserted and the men down on their knees in a hut, praying and with their rifles stacked in a corner, he was gentle with them but told them there was a time for prayer and a time for duty. Finally he slept a few hours himself, on a flour sack on the floor.

The British rapidly established a line across Dublin that cut the Republican line in two, separating the rebel strongpoints so communication was blocked except for reports messengers smuggled through. British cordons were tightened around the Republican positions. Wednesday morning, British field guns from Trinity College and a gunboat on the Liffey River opened a bombardment that demolished already evacuated Liberty Hall. Incendiary shells set other buildings aflame. The top of the Post Office was blown off, but the Republican command held out and the flag still flew.

While the British systematically went about reducing much of downtown Dublin to rubble, citizens swarmed into the streets to loot shops and stores with little regard for their own safety. Wanting their share of good things long denied them, Dublin's poor grabbed clothes, watches, jewelry, golf clubs, sweets from candy shops. Middle class Dubliners, seeing only the collapse of established law and order and the destruction of property, were outraged by the revolution. Many people with sons or relatives fighting beside the British against the Germans denounced the revolutionaries as wartime traitors.

But at the beleaguered Post Office, Pearse issued a manifesto, praising the Republicans killed and wounded, and those who fought on. "Win they will," he said, "although they may win in death. Already they have won a great thing . . .proclaiming the Irish Republic as a Sovereign State. . . . For my part, I am not afraid to face either the judgment of God or the judgment of posterity."

When word reached Republican headquarters that two

thousand British troops from England had landed at Kingstown and were preparing to march on Dublin, two girls, members of the Volunteer auxiliary but dressed in street clothes instead of uniform, managed to sneak through the British lines to warn De Valera. They could bring him no help, but he had time to set the trap around Mount Street Bridge and late Wednesday afternoon eight hundred British soldiers marched into it.

The British Sherwood Foresters, advancing down Northumberland Road, came directly under the crossfire of the fourteen men De Valera had in houses along the approach, and the British tried to storm the bridge by frontal attack. In wave after wave, with rifles, machine guns, incendiary bombs and grenades, they fought for five hours. Hundreds finally overcame the two men in the house a block from the bridge and hundreds more threw themselves at other positions. The six men in Clanwilliam House held out not only against the incoming troops but also against attacks from the city side.

It was night when the British took the bridge, at the terrible cost to them of four officers dead, fourteen officers wounded, and 216 soldiers killed or wounded. Their casualties amounted to nearly half of all those suffered by the British during the entire rebellion. De Valera had lost a total of four men killed. Several others were wounded or taken prisoner.

Boland's was still strongly held and with sniper support De Valera still commanded a large area. British attacks to drive him out of the bakery and mill grew more intense. For three days there was hardly a lull in the firing. The British began shelling the bakery and to divert the artillery attack De Valera sent a few men to a nearby abandoned distillery. Windows were lighted at night, signal flags were waved on the roof in daytime, and rumors were spread to lead the British to believe the distillery had become a rebel headquarters with reinforcements moving in. The British turned their artillery fire from Boland's to the empty distillery and the gunboat *Helga* joined in the bombardment of it from the river.

De Valera had no direct communication with headquarters, no knowledge of what was happening to Republican forces in the rest of Dublin. But the reports he heard were bad. The great explosions in the heart of the city and the orange-red glow of the sky at night told enough.

In downtown Dublin, as the last battles were fought, the Post Office was evacuated and its defenders moved from building to building by breaking through connecting walls until they reached a place from which there was nowhere else to go. Britain's military chief, General Sir John Maxwell, had threatened to powder the city to dust if the opposition went on. Finally, late on Saturday, April 29, Pearse gave the order to surrender "in order to prevent the further slaughter of Dublin citizens, and in the hope of saving the lives of our followers now surrounded and hopelessly outnumbered."

De Valera had never considered surrender. He had taken up his gun to fight or to die for Ireland. His men still held Boland's and he was still fighting when the surrender document was brought to him on Sunday. He had never seen the girl messenger who presented it and at first thought it was a forgery and refused to accept it, until it was confirmed. Even then some of his men wanted to go on fighting, and some smashed their guns rather than give them up to the British.

During the night before, talking to a man tending the bakery delivery wagon horses, De Valera had spoken of the victory for Ireland that might have been if the people had risen together to support the fight for freedom, even with no weapons at all. He had said, "If only the people had come out with knives and forks . . ."

But now he spoke to his men, reminding them they were all soldiers, and that even this bitter decision to surrender had to be obeyed in soldierly manner. With a British prisoner as hostage he made his way through the lines to a nearby hospital, identified himself to a doctor, and waited until a British officer arrived. "Do what you like with me," he told the British Captain, E. J. Hitzen, to whom he surrendered, "but I demand proper treatment for my men."

CHAPTER 5

Exhausted, disheveled, his face stubbled with beard and his green uniform streaked with flour, Commandant De Valera was marched through the streets to prison with his men, flanked by British soldiers with flashing bayonets, but he still walked with his head erect, his eyes defiant, and with no surrender of spirit.

He was kept for a week at the Ballsbridge Barracks, where he had a chance to escape but refused. The window of the room where he was imprisoned opened upon the driveway of a fire brigade station and some of the firemen plotted to get him free. They rolled out the fire engine with its motor racing so he could leap from the window and jump aboard, but De Valera knew his escape might mean harsher punishment for the men who had been jailed with him so he decided to stay in prison.

Rebellion had left three thousand people wounded or dead, many of them civilians. Blocks of central Dublin's buildings, stores and homes lay in bombed and fire-blackened ruin. There was acute suffering, shock and anger, and little sympathy at

first for the revolutionists. Most of the Irish people wanted only
the restoration of law and order and for that they looked to
British authority.

It was the British who changed the feelings of the Irish.
Determined to crush all lingering revolt, they imposed harsh
martial law and in the words of British General Maxwell abandoned "velvet glove methods." In the aftermath of rebellion, it
was British jails and executions that kept alive the Easter
Rising.

While De Valera, the last of the revolutionary commandants
to surrender, was held at Ballsbridge, the British swept hundreds of other prisoners into every jail that could hold them.
All over Ireland they arrested men and women merely suspected of having the slightest Republican sympathy. People
were dragged from homes and businesses at gunpoint. Some
were crowded into bare detention rooms, thirty to a room,
with no facilities to care for them. Tales of new British tyranny
spread through every village until no town in Ireland was
without its local martyr.

Many were brought to Dublin's Kilmainham Prison and to
Richmond Barracks, where they were imprisoned with others
whose revolutionary passions were far greater than their own.
The jails became "universities of revolution" where the doc-
trines and hopes of the leaders of Easter Week inspired men
from every part of Ireland. Before the arrests ended nearly
three thousand Irishmen were jailed, most of them without
trial. Defiantly they talked of continued rebellion, and in their
cells sång *The Soldier's Song* that was to become the Irish
national anthem: "Soldiers are we, whose lives are pledged to
Ireland. . . . Sworn to be free . . ."

On May 3, 1916, with no previous public announcement,
the British began putting the leaders of the Rising to death
before firing squads. The courts martial were held in secret and

nothing was known until the curt official notice was given that Pearse, MacDonagh and T. J. Clarke, three of the signers of the Proclamation, had been tried and "shot this morning."

The next day three more were shot to death, another on the day following, others a day or two apart. Day after day, the grim announcements came, and the public was shocked at each execution. Pearse's brother Willie was put to death not because he had been a leader of the Rising but mainly because his name was Pearse. James Connolly, beloved by Dublin's workers and already dying of battle wounds, had to be carried out on a stretcher to be propped up before the firing squad that shot him. Ninety insurgents secretly were sentenced to die, but public outcry halted the British executions at fourteen.

Most of the courts martial and some of the executions were over before De Valera was transferred from Ballsbridge to Richmond Barracks for trial. On May 8, the day he went on trial, four men were executed. He expected no clemency. After two days of waiting in jail for the verdict, he was informed that he also had been found guilty and would die.

But by then the shots of the British firing squads in Dublin had echoed around the world. English newspapers and speakers in Parliament were calling the executions "atrocities" and were warning that the government was inflaming revolution by making martyrs of the leaders of the Rising.

Among the public protesters was playwright George Bernard Shaw who wrote that "the men who were shot in cold blood, after their capture or surrender, were prisoners of war" and that "it is absolutely impossible to slaughter a man in this position without making him a martyr and a hero." Shaw predicted that the dead Irishmen would take their places beside the great heroes of Irish history and "beside the heroes of Poland and Serbia and Belgium in Europe" and that the British military, by their executions, were "canonizing their prisoners."

In England's colonies, and among Irishmen fighting beside the British in Europe's trenches, there was growing anger. Loudest of all was the rage of protest from Irish-Americans in the United States, where newspapers had published daily extra editions to report each execution in shocking detail. America's wartime help was vital to the British and they became concerned.

De Valera had never claimed American citizenship when he came of age. When he took up arms for Ireland, he renounced all citizenship except to the Irish Republic. But the fact that he had been born in the United States probably weighed in the second thoughts the British had about shooting him to death.

His death sentence was followed by an announcement that it had been commuted. He would not be executed, but he was sentenced instead to serve in prison for the rest of his life. Handcuffed and led under close guard to the Dublin docks, he was put aboard a ship to be deported with many others sentenced with him to English convict prisons.

The British had arrested more Irishmen than they knew what to do with and hundreds, never formally tried or convicted, were crowded into the pens of cattle boats and the holds of freighters to be distributed to various jails in England. Eventually some eighteen hundred were classified as prisoners of war and were transferred to an internment camp in Wales, but De Valera, as a life-term convict, was sent with sixty-four others to England's maximum security prison at Dartmoor.

Thrown in with thieves and other common criminals, confined to cells that were damp and barely lighted, subjected to the monotony of empty hours with no exercise except to circle around the prison yard once a day in measured paces and in forced silence, De Valera and his Irish comrades rebelled. Considering themselves prisoners of war, they were determined to hold themselves apart and demand treatment as captured soldiers and not convicts. Despite the attempt by their jailers to keep them from forming a group, they managed to organize, and as the senior commandant, De Valera became their leader. At his nod or whispered command they constantly challenged prison rules and regulations, in small ways, but in defiance of British authority.

Lined up for inspection with the rest of the convicts in the central hall one morning about a month after they had arrived, the Irishmen were standing in dead silence when they saw a new prisoner being led down the iron stairs and recognized him as Eoin MacNeill, former Commander of the Volunteers, who finally had been tried in Dublin and sentenced to life in prison. They had mixed feelings about him because MacNeill had countermanded the orders for nationwide rebellion, but De Valera, without hesitation, stepped out of the convict ranks, faced his men, and commanded a salute to MacNeill: "Irish Volunteers, attention! Eyes left!"

They obeyed with military precision and De Valera then stepped back into the ranks. His men, as one of them wrote, were "dazed by his chivalry and courage," but his jailers were infuriated. He was marched off to a separate cell for punishment.

When he continued to lead acts of defiance, he was moved to Maidstone Jail. In December, 1916, chained as well as handcuffed, he was transferred from there to Lewes Jail, south of London, where the British finally concentrated all the insurgent Irish convicts. Once again, De Valera became their leader. Letters from prisoners to relatives back home spread the stories about his resistance in jail and his leadership in uniting the men and the Irish people, avid for news of the prisoners, began to find a national hero in De Valera.

Public opinion in Ireland had undergone a dramatic change. The British executions had not only made martyrs of the leaders of the Rising but had fixed them in the historic pattern of centuries-old resistance to British rule. Put to death by the British as Irish patriots always had been, Pearse and Connolly already had become men who would "speak forever." Their words, their writings, the sacrifice of their lives, gave the Irish a sense of purpose, a renewal of pride in nationhood. People who first had been shocked by revolution began to accept the need for it, and became eager to identify themselves with the living survivors of the Rising, men like De Valera who had helped show the way to independence, and who still fought for it even in jail.

All through the summer and fall of 1916 the British went on making daily arrests in Ireland, but the growing spirit of national rebellion fed upon resistance. With thousands of troops pinned down by the troubles in Ireland, the British and their allies were losing heavily on European battlefronts of the World War and there were fears that without fresh manpower from the United States they would be exhausted, perhaps defeated. But in an America that was still hesitant about entering the war, sympathy for the Irish and against the English was becoming so intense that warnings were sent from Washington to urge the government in London to do something about the "Irish problem" so as to make a show of good intentions.

Lloyd George, about to become Britain's Prime Minister, quickly moved to revive the possibility of Home Rule, but hedged with provisions that would partition much of Ulster from the rest of Ireland. At Christmas, after he had taken office, he made another attempt to soothe Irish and American feelings. He ordered the Irish prisoners held in English internment camps, though not De Valera and other convicts, released and sent home.

Men who had been imprisoned for months without trial by the English came back to Ireland by the hundreds, hardened in their determination to set Ireland free. They spread prison-learned methods of rebellion to others in every Irish town and village to which they returned. Six hundred came from the internment camp at Frongoch in Wales, where they had schooled themselves in defying the British, had formed classes to study the Irish language and history, and had kept up their morale by singing the songs of freedom. And many had sworn secret oaths to the Irish Republican Brotherhood.

Among the freed prisoners was Michael Collins, a leader of the resistance at Frongoch and an organizer of the secret society. An ardent, impulsive twenty-seven-year-old veteran of the Easter Rising, with a fund of boisterous humor and a gift of easy comradeship, Collins had hardly set foot in Ireland again before he was at the center of nationalist movements in which his influence swiftly grew. Also among the freed was Arthur Griffith, whose Sinn Fein had expanded far beyond his own ideas in founding it.

De Valera, still imprisoned at Lewes, knew of what was happening at home only from rumors and occasional messages smuggled through, but he was aware of the fact that the Irish Republicans, in February, 1917, had won their first success as a political party. Contesting a by-election in Roscommon for a seat held in the British Parliament by a representative of Redmond's Home Rule Party, they had chosen as their candidate Count Plunkett, father of Joseph Plunkett, executed by the British as one of the signers of the Proclamation of the Irish Republic. Count Plunkett was pledged, if he won, to refuse to take his seat in the British Parliament, and he won by a majority of more than two to one.

Spurred by the victory, the new Sinn Fein party contested a second election in Longford in May, choosing one of the prisoners still in jail at Lewes with De Valera as a candidate. Sinn Fein denounced Home Rule as a smokescreen for the partition of Ireland, and won the election of their Republican convict, Joseph McGuinness.

That same month, in the jail at Lewes, De Valera led his fellow prisoners into an open revolt designed to create an international uproar for their freedom. He once again demanded that authorities treat them as prisoners of war, and when the British refused, stripped them of all prison privileges and ordered them confined to their cells, De Valera commanded his men to break windows and furniture and to refuse to obey any regulations at all. They turned the whole prison into a place of continuing riot.

In an attempt to break up the group, the British removed the Irish prisoners from Lewes and scattered them in small numbers through half a dozen English jails. De Valera and some others were transferred in chains to a prison at Pentonville, but wherever they were sent they continued to revolt. In Ireland meanwhile Sinn Fein had made it clear that it meant to elect more of the absent convicts to seats they would refuse to take in the British Parliament so as to show the people's contempt for English government. When a great protest meeting held in Dublin on behalf of the prisoners was broken up by police who clubbed their way through an angry crowd to arrest speakers, the crowd turned on the police, beat some, and fatally injured a police inspector.

Prime Minister Lloyd George finally decided that keeping De Valera and the others in jail was costing the British government more in support and prestige than it was worth. Seeking to calm the situation in Ireland, with the hope that he could get the people to give up demands for an independent Republic and to discuss proposals for limited self-government under the Empire, he announced on June 15, 1917, that in order to secure a favourable atmosphere for deliberations, Britain would release the remaining Irish prisoners.

De Valera was told that night that he had been reprived from his sentence of life imprisonment. He and his men were to be put aboard a ship to Ireland and freedom the next day. As he left the gates of Pentonville Prison, he was handed a telegram. He had been chosen by Sinn Fein to represent the Republicans in a by-election in County Clare.

Throughout Ireland there was wild rejoicing over the news that De Valera and the prisoners were coming home. Eager Dublin crowds waited up through the night for their arrival, but it was the morning of June 17 before they were landed at Kingstown. As the vessel docked, one hundred prisoners, their hair cropped and their faces pale, lined the rails and joined in singing *The Soldier's Song.* At De Valera's command they formed military ranks and marched behind him in double file down the gangway to the boat-train that would take them into Dublin's Westland Row Station.

There, at the station that De Valera's own battalion had occupied during the Easter Rising, they were officially welcomed by Dublin aldermen, and were paraded in automobiles through the streets of the city to the cheers of surging crowds who had halted all work to make a holiday of the homecoming. Along the streets, where traffic was stopped for the motorcade, there were women and some men who openly wept with joy. For De Valera and the men who had been marched as prisoners through the same streets after the collapse of the Rising when the hope for a Republic seemed to lie in ruins, the emotional welcome was evidence beyond any dream of a great national awakening. He had gone away in defeat and had come back to find a people waiting for him to lead.

That night while bonfires of celebration blazed on the hills of Ireland and its cities and towns echoed to the playing of bands and the making of speeches at public gatherings, De Valera and twenty-four men who had been officers of the

Volunteers sat quietly in a room in Dublin and drafted a message to the President and Congress of the United States. President Wilson had said that no people must be forced to accept "a sovereignty under which it does not wish to live," and had declared that America's entry into the World War on the side of the British was a fight for the right of all peoples to choose their own governments. De Velera now claimed that right for the Irish people in Wilson's own words and his message asked for the help of the United States in achieving recognition of it.

"We, the undersigned, who have been held in English prisons, and have been dragged from dungeon to dungeon in heavy chains . . . are engaged and mean to engage ourselves in the practical means for establishing this right," De Valera wrote. "We . . . are officers . . . of forces formed independently in Ireland to secure the complete liberation of the Irish nation."

CHAPTER 6

Eamon De Valera came home from jail to a family that had grown in his absence with the birth of another son, a boy called Ruairi. It had been a hard time for Sinead and the children while he was imprisoned in England. She had moved from the house at Donnybrook in suburban Dublin to a place near the sea at Greystones, in neighboring Wicklow County south of the revolution-torn city.

There De Valera privately took up his life again, in simple home surroundings that were much the same as if he had gone on in his career as a teacher, but publicly his life would never be the same. He had left the classroom hardly more than a year before, but now he seemed to many to be a man who had suddenly sprung up from nowhere to become the leader of his people. Before long the Irish people would be singing a ballad that ended ". . . and when we next challenge England we'll beat her in the fight. . . . And we'll crown De Valera King of Ireland."

King, he never wanted to be, and perhaps he never really wanted to run for that first election in County Clare. He had never made a political speech from any public platform. It would have been much easier for him to turn back to his school books and his classes. But Sinn Fein had chosen him as its candidate and somebody had to stand up and say, more boldly than anybody had yet dared to say it, that the fight for an Irish Republic had just begun.

There was a tradition in Irish politics that "what County Clare does today Dublin will do tomorrow." De Valera went there early in July, 1917, as a leader of the Easter Rising, a representative of revolution for a Republic, whose election would amount to a protest vote for the complete separation of all Ireland from the British Empire. He was a stranger to Clare's voters and his opponent was a well-known Crown Prosecutor, Patrick Lynch, the candidate of the Irish Parliamentary Party that supported limited Home Rule. The battle, De Valera's backers said, was between the Crown Prosecutor and the "Crown Prosecuted."

De Valera based his speeches for Irish independence on the principles to which Britain and the United States claimed to adhere in fighting the World War, the right of small nations to govern themselves according to the will of their people. Lynch answered that such demands would turn England's guns upon the Irish and that voters would see "their sons shot down in a futile and insane attempt to establish an Irish Republic."

When the votes were counted, De Valera had won such an overwhelming victory that even his opponents admitted the result was a "stupefying blow." In London, the *Daily Express* editorialized that Sinn Fein was "sweeping the country like a tidal wave" and that the Irish Parliamentary Party was being "blotted out . . . completely and, apparently, irretrievably."

Far more important than De Valera's victory in Clare itself were the celebrations and speeches all over Ireland that hailed him as the country's new-found leader. He appeared at a celebration in Dublin, wearing his old uniform as a Commandant of the Volunteers, and told the audience, "This election will always be history—a monument to the glorious men of Easter Week who died for us." But if Ireland hoped to present its case at any coming peace conference of world nations, he went on, it first must claim absolute independence, which would be "only voicing the feelings of every Irish heart."

Dublin Castle responded by ordering a crackdown on "activities disloyal to the British Government." Men were arrested once more for flying the Republican flag, for making remarks "likely to cause disaffection," for singing freedom songs or old Irish ballads that suggested anti-British sentiments, and police invaded plays, concerts and social gatherings to seize people for "unlawful assembly." But the people continued to demonstrate and to cheer the men who openly paraded in the uniform of the resurgent Irish Volunteers.

One thousand Volunteers marched in review before De Valera in County Clare on July 30, and the next day the British issued a military order prohibiting the wearing of unauthorized uniforms in public places and the carrying of any objects that might be used as weapons, "except for some lawful employment or pastime." De Valera, at a public meeting, advised the men to evade the British order by carrying sticks used for the sport of hurley, and to adopt the Volunteer uniform as their habitual work clothes. Armed with their Irish hockey sticks, and still uniformed, Volunteers soon were parading in a dozen counties. When arrested, as some were, they cheerfully paid small fines and went right on marching.

In August there was an election in Kilkenny and De Valera suggested putting up William Cosgrave as the Sinn Fein candidate. Another veteran of the Rising, Cosgrave had been a prisoner in English jails with De Valera and like him had been first sentenced to death and then to a life term in prison before being released. Cosgrave won the Kilkenny election by twice as many votes as his opponent of the Irish Parliamentary Party.

The British reacted to the new Sinn Fein victory by suppressing some newspapers, searching private homes, and jailing more than eighty Republicans. Some of the prisoners went on a hunger strike and one of them, Thomas Ashe, died from wounds suffered during British attempts to force him to eat. A mass meeting of protest in Dublin, led by De Valera, adopted a resolution calling the attention of the United States "to the fact that Irishmen are being arrested . . . and sentenced to long terms of imprisonment for declaring in the words of President Wilson . . . 'that no people shall be forced to live under a sovereignty under which it does not desire to live.' "

Thousands filed past Ashe's coffin as the dead hunger-striker, dressed in his Volunteer uniform, lay in state in Dublin's city hall. He was given a military funeral as a slain soldier of the Republic and thirty thousand people joined in the procession, headed by an honour guard of armed Volunteers, followed by two hundred priests and by delegates from nearly every nationalist organization in Ireland. The Volunteers fired three volleys of shots over Ashe's body as it was lowered into the grave.

When Britain's Prime Minister Lloyd George set up an Irish Convention to suggest proposals for self-government under continued British rule, Sinn Fein and the Irish Labour Party boycotted it as not representing the true aspirations of the Irish people. Sinn Fein called a convention of its own to bring together all the nationalists in one disciplined organization with a clear and definite objective. The *Ard-Fheis*, which was the Irish name for the convention that was to become the governing body of Sinn Fein, met at the Mansion House in Dublin on October 25, 1917.

De Valera became its key figure and worked mightily to

bring together many different factions antagonistic to each other. There were revolutionary Republicans, socialists and Marxists, directly opposed in their views to ultra-conservative nationalists who wanted only a native parliament which would control business and taxes, and there were other delegates who didn't much care what form the government took once the British were ousted.

Arthur Griffith would not bind himself to seeking a Republican form of government. Cathal Brugha, a veteran officer of the Rising and leader of another faction, would have nothing to do with the movement unless it flatly declared itself for a Republic. Michael Collins headed an influential group affiliated with the Irish Republican Brotherhood, which tried to exercise its own control. De Valera himself had become determined to break all connections with the I.R.B., taking the stand that henceforth Sinn Fein should be an open movement with none of its elected representatives subject to secret control.

The differences at first seemed irreconcilable. But De Valera, presiding over the stormy meetings of a pre-convention committee chosen to draw up a Sinn Fein constitution, showed that his leadership ability was not just as a military commander. They all wanted Ireland's freedom, he said, so the real problem was to find a wording that would satisfy all parties. He offered a definition that was accepted and written into the constitution: "Sinn Fein aims at securing the international recognition of Ireland as an independent Irish Republic. Having achieved that status the Irish people may by referendum freely choose their own form of government."

Sinn Fein also pledged itself "in the name of the Sovereign Irish people" to "deny the right and oppose the will of the British Parliament to legislate for Ireland" and to use "any and every means available to render impotent the power of England to hold Ireland in subjection by military force or otherwise."

When the convention's seventeen hundred delegates met, the constitution was unanimously approved. Arthur Griffith, who had fathered the old Sinn Fein and headed it for years, stepped aside for the sake of unity, along with other possible candidates, and De Valera was elected without opposition as president of the new Sinn Fein.

His election, De Valera told the convention, was an endorsement by the Irish nation of the action of the insurgents of the Easter Rising, "proof that they were right" in what they fought for, "the complete and absolute freedom and separation from England," with no contemplation "of having a monarchy in which the monarch would be the House of Windsor." Aware that some of his listeners had different views, he tried to fuse them together by ending with an emotional appeal: "We say it is necessary to be united under the flag under which we are going to fight for our freedom—the flag of the Irish Republic. We have nailed that flag to the mast; we shall never lower it. I ask you to salute that flag . . ."

In the resounding applause, he seemed to have achieved that unity. Three weeks later, the Irish Volunteers, who remained independent of Sinn Fein, met in a separate Army convention and elected De Valera their president, so that he became head of both the civil and military forces of the Irish movement, much to the growing alarm of the British.

De Valera's speeches worried Prime Minister Lloyd George, who told the House of Commons that he had been reading them and had found that "so far as language is concerned they are not violent," but were nevertheless "plain, deliberate . . . incitements to rebellion." Said England's Prime Minister: "He has repeated them in meeting after meeting in almost the same studied terms . . . urging the people to train, to master their rifles. . . . That is not a case of violent, abusive, and excitable language. It is the case of a man of great ability, of considerable influence, deliberately going . . . to stir people up to rebellion against the authorities. . . . The words which are used are 'sovereign independence.' This country could not possibly accept that under any conditions."

Early in April, 1918, the British government inflamed Irish feelings even more. Lloyd George put before Parliament a bill to force Irishmen to serve in the British Army by conscription. At the same time he announced that after conscription was enforced the government would consider some measure of limited Home Rule for the Irish.

The British had good military reasons; on Europe's Western Front the Allies were under such massive attack by the Germans that even the arrival in France of the first troops from the United States did not supply enough reinforcements. But to many of the Irish, the British were the enemy, and now the Irish were being told that first they would be dragged into the British Army, and only then would the British consider giving them some additional freedom of government. Even those who had been most friendly to the idea of Home Rule under the British were outraged by the Conscription Act. They felt that Lloyd George had been dangling Home Rule before them only to bait them into swallowing conscription.

In London the entire Irish Party in Parliament voted against the Conscription Act, and when the bill was passed, the Irish representatives walked out of the House of Commons in protest and returned to Ireland. On April 18, a group representing all shades of Irish political opinion, the Parliamentary Party, Sinn Fein and Labour, met in Dublin and temporarily buried their differences to draw up a pledge that was to be signed by the Irish people at every parish in Ireland the following Sunday.

De Valera worded the pledge and he also drew up a declaration unanimously adopted by all parties at the Dublin meeting: "Taking our stand on Ireland's separate and distinct nationhood and affirming the principle of liberty that the governments of nations derive their just powers from the consent of the governed, we deny the right of the British Government . . . to impose compulsory military service in Ireland against the clearly expressed will of the Irish people. The passage of the Conscription Bill . . . must be regarded as a declaration of war on the Irish nation. The alternative to accepting it as such is to surrender our liberties and to acknowledge ourselves slaves."

He headed a group that appealed to an annual meeting of Catholic bishops for their support and the bishops issued a manifesto against British conscription. Labour meanwhile called a twenty-four-hour general strike that shut down businesses, factories and transportation everywhere in Ireland except in the pro-British city of Belfast.

With De Valera and Sinn Fein, other nationalist groups, labor, the Catholic hierarchy, and even the traditionally cooperative Irish Parliamentary Party turned against them, the British had left themselves no middle ground. They were faced with setting Ireland free, which they would not consider, or with trying to hold it by force.

London ordered the removal from Ireland of nearly all British officials who had shown any sympathy for Irish nationalism. Military officers were shifted. Laws were rewritten to tighten them. The wholesale arrest of leaders of Sinn Fein was carefully plotted. Field Marshal Lord French, veteran commander of expeditionary forces in France and Belgium and formerly Commander-in-Chief of the English Army, was appointed His Majesty's new Lord Lieutenant and Governor of Ireland.

Six days after he took charge, Lord French carried out orders from the British cabinet to jail De Valera and all others prominent in Sinn Fein. On the night of May 17, 1918, and on the day following, arrests were made throughout the country. De Valera was on his way home to Greystones when he was seized. The British claimed to have uncovered a plot, of which no evidence was ever produced, involving Sinn Fein with an attempt by the Germans to invade Ireland with secret agents landed from submarines so as to start another revolution.

Lord French issued a proclamation "that certain subjects of His Majesty the King . . . have conspired to enter into, and have entered into, treasonable communication with the German enemy." He announced that "drastic measures" would have to be taken and appealed to "all loyal subjects of His Majesty" to "aid in crushing the said conspiracy." Michael Collins, Cathal Brugha, and some others managed to evade arrest and hide themselves until the raids were over, but almost all other top leaders of Sinn Fein and senior officers of the Volunteers were swept into the British net.

On the basis of the mythical "German plot," De Valera, Cosgrave, Griffith and some seventy more were immediately deported to England to be imprisoned. Once again, De Valera found himself marched between files of British soldiers, to be put aboard a ship at Kingstown. A crowd had gathered there and as he went up the gangplank for the trip to England and an indefinite term in Lincoln Jail, he turned and said to the Irish people: "Be calm and confident."

❧ ❧

CHAPTER 7

The British had De Valera in jail but they hadn't removed his influence from Ireland. While they had him locked up in England he and the Irish Republicans were winning an election victory that not only established Sinn Fein as the majority party but also as an unofficial government of the Irish nation.

Armistice had ended the First World War and Prime Minister Lloyd George, seeking a vote that would strengthen his government, dissolved the British Parliament and called for a general election in all of Great Britain, including Ireland, in December, 1918. Sinn Fein seized the opportunity to make it a national plebiscite and to create a revolutionary Irish parliament of its own.

Republican candidates simply made use of the British election machinery for their own purposes. In order to enter the election they had to run for seats in the British Parliament. But instead of taking their seats in London they intended to sit in their own self-created assembly in Dublin. As elected representatives of the Irish people they meant to erect a complete Republican

government of Ireland that would exist side by side with the
official British government.

Like De Valera, most of Sinn Fein's candidates were in jail.
He sought election not only in East Clare, where he had won
his first victory, but also in East Mayo, where his opponent
would be John Dillon, leader of the Irish Parliamentary Party.
From his cell in Lincoln Jail, De Valera even tried to send out
an election address to the people, but that was intercepted and
banned by British censors.

Sinn Fein's experienced organizers as well as its leaders
had been imprisoned, its newspapers were suppressed, and the
whole election machinery was in British control. Its speakers
were harrassed, its campaign literature was heavily censored,
and its campaigners worked under constant threat of arrest.
But despite enormous difficulties Sinn Fein managed to put up
a candidate for nearly every constituency in Ireland.

De Valera won in both Clare and Mayo. Throughout Ireland, Sinn Fein captured 73 out of 105 seats. The old Irish
Parliamentary Party, which previously had held most of the
seats, elected only six candidates and was politically extinguished. Pro-British Unionists, with their strength centered
mainly around Belfast, took 26 seats, but polled a majority
only in four of Ulster's nine counties.

The people of all Ireland had voted for Sinn Fein and a
Republic by a majority of seventy percent. No longer could
the British claim that Sinn Fein represented only a small fringe
of fanatic nationalists. As the *London Times* reported: "The
General Election in Ireland was treated by all parties as a
plebiscite and admittedly Sinn Fein swept the country."

America's President Wilson already was in Paris for the
coming Peace Conference, being hailed by Europe's multitudes
as a savior who promised to bring a new democracy to the
world. He had pledged "the settlement of every question,
whether of territory or sovereignty . . . by the people immedi-

ately concerned." The Irish people, by their own direct vote, had now asserted their claim to full independence, and they had great hope that the traditional friendship of the United States would win them a hearing at Paris. But they also realized that America had been Britain's ally in the war and that it would now take more than faith in President Wilson's idealism to present that claim. Britain had no intention of giving Ireland any voice at Paris.

With all its might Britain meant to crush what was to the British an illegal rebel Irish Republic. Armed conflict between Republican Ireland and Imperial Britain had become inevitable. De Valera was Ireland's leader and his people needed him. He decided he could no longer remain locked away in Lincoln Jail where the British wanted to keep him.

He plotted his escape for weeks with the help of friends in Ireland through an exchange of secret messages. During his stay in Lincoln Jail he had managed to win some freedom of movement and had lulled his jailers into relaxing their strict watch over him. Every morning he helped the prison's Catholic chaplain at Mass, and he discovered that the chaplain was in the habit of leaving his keys on a table where there were also altar candles which would provide the wax to make an impression of a key. De Valera soon had the wax model he wanted, of a key to a side gate in one of the prison walls, away from the main entrance. But he had no tools or materials for making the key itself.

He sent a postcard off to friends in Dublin and the prison censors passed it through. On it there was a joking message about being locked behind prison bars, and also a humorous drawing of a key, which actually was a tracing from the wax impression. In Dublin, his friends got the meaning of the message. They made a key to the size of the postcard drawing and baked it into a cake which was sent back to the English jail as a gift for one of the other prisoners. The key turned out to be too small, but after another exchange of messages a second cake was sent. It contained not only a key but also a file to shape it to the exact size required.

Michael Collins, who personally took a hand in making the cake before it was shipped from Dublin, had risen to a position of great influence in Sinn Fein as reorganizer of the secret Irish Republican Brotherhood and had built a highly-effective Irish spy system that spread over Ireland and into England and America as well. Collins and Harry Boland came to England to supervise the outside arrangements for De Valera's escape. Wanting to be sure there would be no slip-up, Collins had made a duplicate of the key.

On the night of February 3, 1919, Collins, Boland and another man waited in the dark yard behind Lincoln Jail for a prearranged signal light to be flashed from a prison window. Nearby they had a car to spirit De Valera away. When the signal was flashed, Collins moved up to the gate, put the duplicate key he had brought with him into the lock, and started to turn it. At the same moment De Valera and two fellow Irish prisoners approached the gate from inside.

But as Collins turned his key, it snapped and broke. All the plans, the escape, seemed lost. Collins whispered, "Dev, I've broken the key in the lock!"

Luck was with De Valera. From the inside, he used his own key, pushed it into the lock and poked it around until the broken piece of the other key fell out. He turned the lock open and stepped out to freedom. A relay of cars arranged by Collins hurried him through the night to Manchester, to a house where he was hidden while the news of his escape created a world sensation.

Newspapers published rumours that De Valera had been sighted in various European cities, that he had escaped by boat to some remote island, that he had been flown across the Channel to France to confront President Wilson in person, that he was dead. In the House of Commons there were angry questions.

While British detectives combed England and Ireland for him, the new Republican government meanwhile was created in Dublin. In De Valera's absence twenty-six of the Republicans who had been elected by the people in the December election had convened their first parliament, the Dail Eireann (Assembly of Ireland), at a two-hour meeting in the Mansion House on January 21, 1919. The others who had been elected were still in English jails and as the roll was called each man not there was answered for: "Imprisoned by the foreign enemy."

Although it was all entirely illegal as far as the British were concerned, the meeting was public and foreign visitors and news correspondents filled the gallery. With Cathal Brugha presiding, the Dail members stood and solemnly adopted an Irish Declaration of Independence, reaffirming the Proclamation of the Republic that had been made at the start of the Easter Rising in 1916. "Deputies, you understand from what is asserted in this Declaration," Brugha said, "that we are now done with England. Let the world know it and those who are concerned bear it in mind."

De Valera remained in hiding for a month after his February escape from Lincoln Jail, moving from place to place while the British searched for him. But with the war ended the British government was finding it hard to convince the world that it had sufficient legal excuse to keep the leaders of Sinn Fein in jail, especially since many of them had been elected members of Britain's own Parliament. Demands for their release increased in both England and America. Some of the jailed had been stricken with influenza as a near-epidemic of the disease ravaged the jails, and one of the convicts who had won a seat in the Irish election died on March 6. That night the British House of Commons voted the release of the Irish prisoners.

De Valera once more took his place openly in Ireland as

president of Sinn Fein and of the Volunteers, and when the Dail held its second session early in April he also was declared its President. He strengthened the unity of the movement by choosing a cabinet that represented a wide range of differing nationalist views. He appointed Arthur Griffith his Minister of Home Affairs, Count Plunkett for Foreign Affairs, Cathal Brugha for Defence, Countess Constance Markievicz for Labour, Eoin MacNeill for Industry, William Cosgrave for Local Government, and Michael Collins as Minister of Finance. Richard Mulcahy was made Chief of Staff of the Republic's armed forces.

Collins was put in charge of a campaign to fund the Republic through an issue of bonds that were to be sold to the public and although the British immediately suppressed newspaper advertisements for the bonds he eventually succeeded in raising most of the money. It was to be used for "propagating the Irish case all over the world," to develop foreign trade, promote home industry, sea and land conservation projects, and to establish a separate court system and the framework of an entire independent government.

"There is in Ireland at this moment only one legal authority," De Valera claimed at a session of Dail Eireann early in April, "and that authority is the elected Government of the Irish Republic. . . . Our attitude towards the powers that maintain themselves here against the expressed will of the people shall be this: We shall conduct ourselves towards them in such a way as will make it clear to the world that we acknowledge no rights of theirs. Such use of their laws as we shall make will be dictated solely by necessity and only in so far as we deem them for the public good."

Already there had been minor armed clashes between the Irish Republicans and the British. The Irish Volunteers, under their own constitution, were a body separate from the Republican government, bound to obey only their executive officers, but liaison was maintained by the fact that De Valera was both president of the Volunteers and of the Dail. Republican military Chief of Staff Richard Mulcahy was charged with forming a Republican Army but as yet there was no unified control. Minister of Defense Cathal Brugha advocated a strong policy of armed resistance to the British and Michael Collins sometimes wanted to go beyond even what Brugha approved. With military councils divided, local Volunteer companies often made their own decisions.

In Tipperary County a small band of Volunteers ambushed a cart of explosives being escorted by an armed guard of police. The police raised their rifles to fire and the Volunteers shot two of them to death and escaped with the explosives. British reprisals inflamed the situation and soon there were other clashes. Guerilla warfare that gradually would spread over all of Ireland had begun.

On both sides there was a gathering of force through the spring of 1919. The Volunteers, desperately in need of arms and explosives, started raiding British patrols and barracks to get them. They set up a secret munitions factory in Dublin. In still isolated incidents there were British killings of Irishmen and Irish killings of British. Tanks, armored cars, and soldiers with bayonets patrolled Irish cities. Police and military raids were answered with raids by the Irish. In the making was the full revolution that was to burst into a War for Irish Independence.

De Valera looked to Ireland's friends in the United States for the two things it immediately needed most: world recognition of the Irish Republican government and money to support a war for its defense. In Washington the United States Senate had adopted a resolution calling on President Wilson to use his great influence to get a hearing for De Valera and other Irish spokesmen at the Peace Conference at Versailles.

But President Wilson informed Irish representatives in Paris that the Allies had decided no small nationality group should be heard without the unanimous consent of the Four Powers. Great Britain, of course, would not consent. The British were not about to let De Valera use Versailles as a platform from which he could speak to the world about Irish freedom.

De Valera decided the United States itself offered him his best platform. He could speak freely there with the knowledge that what he said would be reported all over the world. There was no other place, outside Ireland, where the feeling for Irish independence was stronger than in America. He made up his mind to go to the United States, to make a direct appeal to the sympathetic American people for funds, to the American nation for moral support, and to the American government for recognition.

The British didn't want De Valera in Ireland; they didn't want him in Paris; least of all, did they want him in the United States. They wouldn't let him leave Dublin freely to visit America. British intelligence officers had to be outwitted. Collins worked out the plans.

Arrangements were made for De Valera to go secretly from Ireland to England. In Liverpool, dressed as a longshoreman, he mixed with a crowd of workers boarding the steamship *Lapland*. Once aboard, he was hidden away below decks in a small utility room, and with the connivance of Irish sailors he made the passage to America as a stowaway.

It had been thirty-four years since he had left his birthplace, New York. On June 11, 1919, his ship entered New York harbor. That night he was secretly taken ashore, but his arrival was not revealed for almost two weeks. In Dublin, on June 17, Arthur Griffith informed the Dail: "The President has, by and with the advice of the Ministry, gone on a mission abroad."

CHAPTER 8

De Valera traveled around secretly for twelve days, conferring with Irish-American leaders in New York, Philadelphia and elsewhere, and visiting Rochester, New York, for a reunion with his elderly mother, before he dramatically appeared in midtown Manhattan to reveal his presence in the United States.

World speculation as to his whereabouts ended with the announcement that he would hold a press conference the evening of June 23, 1919, at the old Waldorf-Astoria Hotel. Shortly after five o'clock a black sedan drew up to the entrance and De Valera "appeared from nowhere" to the shouted welcome of a crowd that jammed Fifth Avenue for a glimpse of him. Wearing glasses, dressed in a dark suit, he looked every inch a dignified visiting chief of state.

"From today I am in America as the official head of the Republic established by the will of the Irish people in accordance with the principles of self-determination," he told fifty news correspondents. "I come here entitled to speak for the Irish nation with an authority democratically as sound and as

well based as that with which President Wilson speaks for the
United States or Lloyd George for England."

A reporter asked if he were an American citizen and he
answered decisively, "No, I am a citizen of Ireland." Another
wanted to know if it were true that he had arrived by submarine, but to protect those who had helped him he gave no
explanations. He was here; that was all he would say. He was
in the United States "to tell the people of America the truth
about Ireland."

Drawing a parallel between the American Revolution and
Ireland's, he said, "The very same catch-cries and the very same
tools were used by the English government against the leaders
of the American Revolution as are being used today against
us. . . . They fought. We have fought and are still fighting. They
were called traitors and murderers—so are we . . ."

His mission in the United States, in addition to answering
British propaganda and winning American friendship, was to
raise ten million dollars. Subscriptions would be solicited for
bond certificates that could be redeemed at full value with
interest "when the Republic wins recognition and is freed from
the military control of England."

De Valera began his speaking tour in New England a week
later, and was greeted everywhere by cheering crowds. People
waved the Stars and Stripes and the flag of Ireland, shouted
"Long live President De Valera and the Irish Republic," invited
him to address legislatures. Governors and mayors welcomed
him, and in New Hampshire he was carried to a platform
while a band played the American presidential salute, *Hail to
the Chief.*

America had found a popular new hero and newspapers
soon jokingly commented that the enthusiasm for De Valera
was so great he "might well find himself elected President of
the United States." Cartoonists pictured him shaking hands

with an Uncle Sam who was saying, "I, too, had to fight John Bull for my independence."

On July 10, he addressed an overflow crowd at New York's Madison Square Garden, and started a trip across the country to the West Coast, with official receptions, banquets, dinners, and a showering of civic scrolls and college degrees along the way. Some 40,000 people jammed the Cubs' baseball field to hear him in Chicago. He spoke to half a million people in California, Utah and Montana.

"The issue raised by the Irish question is a world issue," he declared, "an issue of right and liberty against might everywhere." Reported around the world, his speeches stirred particular interest in India, Africa and some other parts of the British Empire. "History tells us that all great Empires die," he said. "To make Ireland free all that need fall is a ramshackle Empire in which a comparatively small group is keeping millions of people in slavery..."

In Ireland, in September, 1919, the British declared their intention to wipe out the self-proclaimed Republic by force. On September 10, the British officially suppressed the Republican government and parliament. Dail Eireann was declared a "dangerous association" and was prohibited by law. The decree gave the British added sanction to use force and Ireland's rebellion became an active guerilla war of revolution. The outlawed Republican government continued to operate, with difficulty, but with the fighting support of the Irish people.

"England, that went to war 'to make the world safe for democracy,'" De Valera said, when he learned the news, "has this week suppressed the Irish Parliament, a body elected by eighty percent of the votes of the people of Ireland." To many Americans the suppression of Dail Eireann seemed to demonstrate the truth of all that De Valera had been telling them. With bond sales booming on the wave of fresh American

sympathy, he started a second speaking tour to circle the
United States.

In Richmond, he told America's oldest legislative body, the
Virginia Assembly, that the Irish people were one with Patrick
Henry in saying, "Give me liberty or give me death." Squads
of motorcycle police escorted him through the cities of New
Jersey. Railroad lines put on extra trains to accomodate crowds
that came out to welcome him in Pennsylvania. At Philadelphia's Independence Hall, with his hand resting upon the
Liberty Bell, he said, "This shrine is not a shrine for America
alone. It is the shrine of freedom that is America's and that,
God grant, may be Ireland's. It is the symbol of liberty to all
the world."

Cleveland sent out airplanes as well as a procession of automobiles to lead him into the city to the firing of a twenty-one-
gun salute. At an American Indian reservation at Spooner,
Wisconsin, he was made an honarary chief of the Chippewa
Indians. All through the Midwest and on to Colorado, Idaho
and again to California and back, De Valera was welcomed
with the sort of demonstrations usually given a touring President of the United States.

There also were boos as well as cheers, attacks, denuncia-
tions in some newspapers. Prominent British speakers and
American conservatives called him a destroyer of established
government. While he was speaking in Detroit, the British tried
to draw away some of his audience by staging rival celebrations
across the river in Windsor, Ontario, for the Prince of Wales. A
strong Irish-American group opposed De Valera with declarations that "there is no Irish Republic."

But his cross-country tours and the months of speeches that
followed helped give his Irish Republic world stature if not
recognition. In the United States, as he had hoped, he had
found his platform to present Ireland's claim before the world,

and the opportunity to voice the arguments Lloyd George and President Wilson would not let him make at Versailles. He had won Ireland more friends in America than any man ever had and he had raised the millions of dollars more urgently needed now than ever for Ireland's War of Independence.

Late in December, 1919, Lloyd George introduced a plan into the British House of Commons for the partition of Ireland. His proposal for the "Better Government of Ireland" was to write into law what had long been the threat to divide Ireland into separate British governments for the North and South. In theory, each government might send an equal number of representatives to an All-Ireland Council, but the plan called for one parliament for the six Northeastern counties of Ulster, a second parliament for the remaining twenty-six counties of the country, and for restricting the powers of both Irish parliaments so that the supremacy of the British Parliament was preserved.

"We have fought for and we demand an independent Ireland, an Irish Republic for the whole island," De Valera answered from the United States. "We will not sell or barter our birthright for a mess of pottage after an agony of seven hundred years."

The Irish people answered for themselves two weeks later when municipal elections throughout Ireland in January, 1920, swept Sinn Fein into control of local government in almost every large town except Belfast. Even in the six counties of Ulster, Sinn Fein won in two, leaving the Unionists with a majority only in four.

By every means available Sinn Fein now meant to make Ireland ungovernable for the British. Control of the judicial system was captured with the setting up of rival Republican civil and criminal courts. Ignoring the Crown Courts, the people accepted the verdicts of the Sinn Fein courts. In every possible area of government the Irish attempted to ignore British authority as if it no longer existed.

De Valera kept in close touch with his government at home through frequent messages from Arthur Griffith, Michael Collins and others. In his absence Collins had become the effective leader of the growing revolution and Griffith the acting head of government. De Valera was advised that it was vital for him to remain in the United States to keep the Irish question an international issue because, as Griffith put it, America was "the center of gravity of the political situation."

He stayed almost through the year of 1920, while the fighting in Ireland became a time of horror, but in December De Valera finally left the United States as secretly as he had come. President Wilson, voted out of office, was a dying man, and Warren Harding, who would succeed him, was even less likely to grant the Irish Republic the American government's official recognition. De Valera had accomplished much, but there was no more to be gained in America.

Without passport or ticket, but again with the prearranged help of some of the crew, he sailed out of New York aboard the liner *Celtic* for Liverpool. British secret agents guessed he was aboard some ship on the Atlantic and when the *Celtic* docked in England detectives boarded it as part of a routine search of all arriving vessels. Hidden behind sacks of potatoes in a storeroom, De Valera waited out the search and the questioning of other passengers. At dawn, dressed in the rough clothing of a sailor, the President of the Irish Republic got ashore and reached friends who had arranged his secret passage from there to Ireland. He finally arrived in war-torn Dublin on Christmas Eve.

CHAPTER 9

President De Valera established his office at the start of 1921 in a concealed room of a private house in Dublin, well-hidden from the British, and soon was working eighteen hours a day running his outlawed Republican government in the midst of raging war. His cabinet ministers also were in hiding and the suppressed Dail, reduced in numbers, had to hold its sessions in secret at various other private homes. But De Valera kept his government fully functioning in all departments, so it remained the operating government of the people, which he and its other leaders hoped to force the British to recognize as the *de facto* Government of Ireland.

Meanwhile its fighting forces were determined to make military operations in Ireland so costly for the British, in both men and money, that Lloyd George would come to terms. The British were equally determined to strike such terror into the hearts of the Irish that they would accept what was already offered and give up the Republic.

Against fifteen thousand Irish Volunteers, only about three thousand of whom were armed with rifles and revolvers, stood the might of fifty thousand British troops with artillery, tanks and armored cars, plus thousands of police of the Royal Irish Constabulary. But the Volunteers fought a guerilla war that shattered England's pose before the world of merely trying to "pacify" the Irish people.

Volunteers operating as "flying columns," small home-based units of men who wore no identifying uniforms, roamed the hills to strike in surprise attack at British convoys and installations, with their strength in ambush, not pitched battle. In the cities it was a war of street shootings and assassination, with armed raiders smashing their way into homes, and murderously dirty fighting on both sides.

Michael Collins, who had become the real commander and driving force of military operations against the British, also personally directed a twelve-man Irish "execution squad" that dramatically crippled the British intelligence system. His "apostles of death" removed dangerous Dublin Castle detectives, secret agents, spies and officials by shooting them down, often in broad daylight, and his own informers infiltrated British police and military organizations, shipping companies, the civil service, and even the War Office in London.

In reprisal for Irish assassinations, British troops fired at random into Irish street crowds. British arrests multiplied into the hundreds. There were jail-yard executions, hunger strikes by prisoners against brutal treatment. Silenced at night by strict curfew, Dublin's streets echoed to the menacing rumble of armored cars and sudden shouts of alarm as bayonet-wielding British raiders prowled through homes for suspects. Men on both sides were shot to death in their beds, children were bullied, women terrorized.

Britain's answer to guerilla warfare was to recruit irregular forces of its own, "the roughest, toughest men in all England," with orders to "make life for the rebels hell." Thousands of former British soldiers and officers, plus some ex-convicts drained out of slums and jails, were recruited through newspaper advertisements in England. When the first of them arrived, there were no regular uniforms for them, so they were dressed in khaki with black caps and belts and soon were called "Black-and-Tans," nicknamed for Irish hound dogs.

Within a month they shot up and sacked some twenty-five towns. They went on to burn half the city of Cork, destroy sixty cooperative creameries, bomb fisheries, rob shops and banks, hold up women on the streets, and generally to flog, beat and murder the Irish. They also aroused world indignation and struck hard at the conscience of the English people themselves.

Lloyd George admitted there had been "deplorable excesses" because "some undesirables" had gotten into the force, but claimed that on the whole the Black-and-Tans were "gallant men." He insisted that the troubles in Ireland were caused by a "small body of assassins, a real murder gang, dominating the country and terrorizing it," and promised that the British soon would have the rebels under control and would have "murder by the throat."

De Valera sent a letter to every member of the British House of Commons, charging each of them individually and all of them collectively with waging full-scale war against the Irish Republic, not merely carrying out a "police action." With approval of the Dail, to counteract British propaganda, he announced that the Volunteers had been formed into the Irish Republican Army as an organized military arm of the Republic, under the civil control of its elected representatives, a "national army of defense," with the government taking full responsibility for all its operations.

By formalizing the Army's status he also hoped to smooth out some of the frictions among his government's leaders.

There had been conflicts between Collins, impatient with official routine, and Defense Minister Cathal Brugha, officially in charge of Army matters, as well as between Collins and Minister of Justice Austin Stack.

De Valera held a press conference with reporters of international news agencies, who kept a promise given in advance to protect his safety by not revealing where they met, and defended the ambushing of British forces by Irish soldiers. "The English forces are in our country as invaders," he said, "waging upon us not only an unjust but a barbarous war. Protected by the most modern war appliances, they swoop down upon us and kill and burn and loot and outrage. . . . If they may use their tanks and steel-armoured cars, why should we hesitate to use the cover of stone walls and ditches? Why should the element of surprise be denied to us? For us not to use it if we proposed defending ourselves at all would be stupid."

With the Republican Army and the British still shooting at each other and the war at its peak, the Irish people went to the polls in May, 1921. The Better Government of Ireland Act, adopted by the British Parliament, came into force, and elections were called for the Act's proposed separate parliaments of Northern and Southern Ireland and for representatives both were to send to the supreme Parliament in London.

De Valera announced that Sinn Fein would put up candidates for all of Ireland, North and South, to show that the combined majority of the Irish people were against partition of the country. For Sinn Fein, it would be an election not to any of the parliaments under the British law but of the people's chosen representatives to a Second Dail Eireann. Those elected would constitute the new Republican Dail.

Those who voted for Sinn Fein, he declared, would be voting "for Ireland against England, for freedom against slavery, for right and justice against force and wrong." At issue was "nothing less than the legitimacy of the Republic," he said. "We are advancing steadily to the final settlement. The blossoms are not the fruit, but the precursors of the fruit—beware how you pluck them."

He ran for election himself not only in the South's County Clare but also in the North's County Down. In the twenty-six counties of the South, election was hardly necessary. The people of every county united solidly behind Sinn Fein and its 124 candidates, including De Valera, were elected without opposition. When the Dublin parliament created by the British law was called into session a month later not a single Sinn Fein representative attended and for all practical purposes it died fifteen minutes after it began.

But in the North's six counties the results were different. De Valera won his contest there and so did nine other Sinn Feiners, but the rest of the 52 seats in Ulster were won by the Unionists. Ulster overwhelmingly voted for partition and to remain part of Britain, with a separate parliament for Northern Ireland of which Sir James Craig became Prime Minister. Inflamed by the riotous campaigning, Ulster's Protestant Volunteers turned against the Catholics to drive them from homes and jobs and "to expel Sinn Fein bag and baggage from the North." Five thousand Catholics were driven out of jobs in shipyards, property was destroyed, and before months of battling in Northern Ireland ended a total of 455 people on both sides had been killed and more than two thousand wounded.

However, in Ireland as a whole the victory clearly was Sinn Fein's, and British Prime Minister Lloyd George no longer could claim the British were fighting only a "small body of assassins." He admitted publicly that "two-thirds of the population of Ireland demand the setting up of an independent Republic" and that "at the recent election they have reaffirmed their demand and have emphatically stated they will agree to nothing else." That meant that any peaceful settlement with the Irish "is in my judgment impossible," he said, "so long as the leaders of Sinn Fein stand in this position and receive the support of their countrymen."

Yet the terrible alternative for the British was to hurl the full military might of the Empire against the Irish in an all-out war of extermination. British military commanders estimated that perhaps 100,000 troops would be needed, and it was becoming clear to Lloyd George and his government that the English people themselves would not stand for such a war, added to the casualties of the World War that already had cost them dearly in money and lives.

Public opinion in England was turning sharply against what opposition speakers in Parliament were calling the government's "criminally cruel and inhuman policy" in Ireland. There were disturbing echoes in India and Africa. The English press and clergy joined in protests. Within Lloyd George's cabinet, policy debates became furious. Concessions were discussed, even the possibility of Dominion status for Ireland. Winston Churchill, then Colonial Secretary, advocated "the fairest offer combined with the most drastic threats."

Lloyd George was unwilling to make any concessions at the cost of his country's prestige or his own. Having promised to "pluck the last revolver from the last assassin's hand," he was reluctant to deal with Sinn Fein in any way until there was a surrender of arms. But he did begin to put out peace feelers. British interests unofficially sounded out Irish Republicans in Dublin to learn what, if any, compromises could be reached as a start toward possible negotiations.

Some quiet soundings were made by Britain's Assistant Undersecretary for Ireland, Alfred Cope. Britain's Lord Derby, wearing horned-rimmed spectacles as a disguise and traveling under the name of "Mr. Edwards," came to talk secretly with De Valera, and to hint that Lloyd George might be willing to consider some form of limited Dominion government for Ireland. De Valera insisted Ireland would accept nothing less than full independence, but there was an exchange of letters between them after Lord Derby returned to London and reported to Lloyd George. The Prime Minister soon told a newspaper interviewer that "I will meet Mr. De Valera . . . without condition on my part," and De Valera told another reporter in Dublin, "If Mr. Lloyd George makes that statement in public, I shall give him a public reply."

Nothing more came of the exchange. Lloyd George was not willing to put himself on record as formally inviting "unconditional" negotiations unless the Irish were willing to accept Dominion status if it were offered. De Valera warily avoided being led into any secret commitments. "The best line to pursue is to indicate they are going on the wrong track," he told an aide, "and that the right way is for them to propose a treaty, with Ireland regarded as a separate state."

De Valera had Irish representatives in London talk to South African statesman Jan Christiaan Smuts, who was in the British capital to attend a coming Dominion conference, and Smuts had a talk about the Irish problem with Britain's King George. In Dublin, there was also a secret meeting between De Valera and Sir James Craig, new Prime Minister of partitioned Northern Ireland, but both were drawn into it on the understanding that each wanted to meet the other, and with their positions on Ulster directly opposite, they found they had nothing to say that could change their views. Despite all sorts of unofficial peace feelers, real negotiations for any meeting between the British and the Irish were at a standstill.

King George broke the deadlock. The King was about to visit Belfast for the opening of the first session of Ulster's new parliament on June 22, 1921. His planned visit was being hailed by Unionists as a symbolic act that once and for all would tie Ulster to the Empire and that might signal the start of all-out war to crush the Irish Republicans in the South and bring the whole country back to the Crown. There was renewed talk in London of fighting the war with the Irish to the end. Rumor had it that the King's coming to Belfast would be followed by sending thousands of British troops across the border into the South.

King George, who had long deplored the troubles in Ireland, had other views and he also possessed the humanity to act upon them. In an act rare for a modern monarch, he personally intervened to put the august majesty of the Crown itself on the side of peace. King George discarded the routine speech that had been written for him and privately summoned General Smuts to help him write a new speech. When he spoke in Belfast, he made a direct personal and emotional appeal for negotiations to end the Irish War.

"I speak from a full heart when I pray that my coming to Ireland today may prove to be the first step towards the end of strife among her people, whatever their race or creed," the King said. "In that hope I appeal to all Irishmen to pause, to stretch out the hand of forbearance and conciliation, to forgive and forget, and to join in making for the land they love a new era of peace, contentment and goodwill . . ."

The King's private secretary meanwhile brought Prime Minister Lloyd George a message that the time had come, without delay, to try to bring about a reconciliation with Ireland. An offer should be made at once, on the strength of the King's speech in Belfast. The Prime Minister and his cabinet held hurried consultations, and as Winston Churchill later wrote, "No British government in modern times has ever appeared to make so sudden and complete a reversal of policy."

Lloyd George had told Parliament only days before that there was no immediate chance of negotiations with Ireland. Two days after the King's speech in Belfast, he wrote De Valera a letter, publicly inviting him to a conference of peace:

"The British Government are anxious that, so far as they can assure it, the King's appeal for reconciliation shall not have been made in vain. . . . I write, therefore, to convey the following invitation to you as the chosen leader of the great majority in Southern Ireland, and to Sir James Craig, the Premier of Northern Ireland, that you should attend a conference here in London . . . to explore to the utmost the possibility of a settlement . . ."

Lloyd George promised that Britain would guarantee "safe conduct" for De Valera and "any colleagues whom you may select." But ironically, on the afternoon that King George delivered his speech in Belfast, De Valera had been arrested by British police in Dublin. They were unaware of his identity when they raided a house in the suburbs and took him prisoner. It wasn't until they brought him to Dublin Castle for questioning that he was identified as the long-hunted President of the Irish Republic.

There were some red faces then. The last thing the British wanted at the moment was De Valera in jail. He, in turn, had no knowledge of the hurried cabinet decisions that were being made in London. Much to his amazement, he found himself released from jail almost immediately. He didn't know why until he received Lloyd George's letter.

CHAPTER 10

De Valera was in no hurry to accept Lloyd George's invitation because it implied conditions he could not accept. He answered promptly that he earnestly wished "to help in bringing about a lasting peace between the peoples of these two islands," but told the British Prime Minister that he saw "no avenue by which it can be reached if you deny Ireland's essential unity and set aside the principle of national self-determination."

He would accept no invitation merely as the leader of a separate Southern Ireland. If he went to London it would be as President of the Republic which stood for an independent people's government of the whole of Ireland, not a partitioned North and South. More than that, before there was any London conference, he wanted a truce in the fighting, but no surrender of arms by the Irish.

De Valera set up new Presidential headquarters at the Mansion House in Dublin, where he was joined by Arthur Griffith who had been released from prison by the British. He called for a conference there on July 4 to discuss the reply he should make to Lloyd George "as spokesman for the Irish nation," and invited five leading Unionists to attend, including Northern Ireland's Prime Minister Sir James Craig. Craig refused to have anything to do with De Valera's Dublin conference, but the four other Unionists accepted.

The Stars and Stripes of the United States, not the Republican tricolor or the British Union Jack, flew from the front of the Mansion House when the Dublin meeting began. Since July 4 was America's Independence Day, De Valera had ordered the American flag honored "as the recognized symbol throughout the world of the principle for which we are fighting —that 'governments derive their just powers from the consent of the governed.' "

On July 9, a truce was announced, to go into effect two days later, and hostilities in Ireland were suspended. Lloyd George, after refusing at first, had given in to De Valera's demand that the Irish be allowed to keep their arms during the truce.

The British agreed not to bring in additional troops or munitions, to lift restrictions on the Republican government, and to guarantee the Irish people their civil rights and freedom of movement. On their part, the Irish agreed to cease attacks on Crown forces, to make no displays of armed force, not to interfere with government or private property, and to take no "action likely to cause disturbance of the peace."

De Valera told the Irish people the truce did not mean victory, but just a start toward negotiations and that "history, particularly our own history, and the character of the issue to be decided are a warning against undue confidence." In his proclamation of the truce, he said, "Should force be resumed against our nation, you must be ready on your part once more to resist . . ."

But it was a warning hardly heard by Ireland's overjoyed people. After months of terror and suffering, there was sudden release, a return to normal living, free of killing and fear. They sang, danced in the streets, waved their flags, cheered for De Valera and the Republic. To most Irishmen the fact that the British had been forced to lay down their guns without any Irish surrender was victory enough. They fervently wanted peace and thought they had it; few among them were in any mood to think the truce might not mean a final settlement.

De Valera telegraphed Lloyd George that he was now ready to meet and discuss "on what basis such a conference as that proposed can reasonably hope to achieve the object desired." Lloyd George invited him to come to 10 Downing Street and De Valera agreed to be there by July 14.

He took with him to London his Vice-President Arthur Griffith, Economic Minister Robert Barton, Home Affairs Minister Austin Stack, and Publicity Minister Erskine Childers. But the meetings were between De Valera and Lloyd George alone, with no representatives of either side present, although both conferred with their colleagues after each session together.

De Valera was not impressed by Lloyd George's outward affability and rather obvious attempts to flatter him, and Lloyd George found De Valera a difficult man to deal with. Negotiating with him, the Prime Minister remarked to an aide, was "like trying to pick up mercury with a fork." When the comment was passed along to De Valera, he said, "Why doesn't he try a spoon?"

The first of their four interviews was held July 14 in the Cabinet Room where chairs had been arranged around a big table for the British Commonwealth Conference that had been holding sessions in the same room. Pointing to a vast map of the world on the wall, Lloyd George talked of the changing relationship between the colonies and the Mother Country and of the growing importance of the Dominion Premiers. He rolled off the names of great men who had sat in those chairs in

Imperial Conference. Twice Lloyd George paused as he came to one particular empty chair and then passed it by to talk about who occupied the others. He seemed to be waiting for De Valera to ask who would sit in that chair, but De Valera refused to rise to the bait. Finally Lloyd George said, "One chair remains vacant, waiting for Ireland . . . if she is ready to take her place in the Council Chamber of the Commonwealth."

De Valera answered that what he wanted was a united Irish nation free to determine its own affairs. By the end of their second interview he was convinced they were getting nowhere and that the British meant to offer Ireland only limited Dominion Home Rule. He pressed Lloyd George at their third talk to put the British terms in writing and after some debate the Prime Minister agreed and they were delivered to De Valera's hotel the night of July 20.

What the British proposed was a Dominion in which they would keep naval control of Irish seas, coasts and harbors, limit the size of Irish military forces, recruit troops for the British Army, charge Ireland for a share of Britain's World War debts, and expect allegiance to the King. They expressed the hope that Ulster would join in a united Ireland, but said the North could not be forced to unite with the South and would have to consent by its own free decision in "full recognition of the existing powers and privileges of the Parliament of Northern Ireland."

De Valera tossed the document on the table when he saw Lloyd George the next day and said he could never agree to such terms and would not even carry them back to the Irish people. In that case, Lloyd George threatened, there would be renewed war and "the responsibility for it will rest on your shoulders." De Valera answered that it would be Britain the world would blame "if you insist on attacking us."

The Prime Minister then threatened to brush aside an agreement they had made to keep the discussions private and said he would publish the British terms. De Valera told him to go ahead and that he would publish his reasons for refusing so that the Irish people would understand.

He started to walk out of the room, but Lloyd George stopped him at the door and asked if he would not give a more considered answer. He would, De Valera said, if Lloyd George would keep his original promise and not publish the proposals until there was time for a full consultation in Dublin. Lloyd George agreed. De Valera left the document on the table, still refusing to carry it back to Ireland himself, but a copy was forwarded by the British.

In Dublin the Irish leaders reportedly were divided during their informal discussions, with Collins and Griffith taking the view that while the British offer was not what they wanted it was a step in the right direction. Whatever their private views, however, all the ministers at a full meeting turned down the British proposals, and the new Dail, meeting in August, unanimously and officially confirmed De Valera's stand and also unanimously reelected him President.

He announced that he was reducing his ministry to a more workable small cabinet, in which Griffith would handle foreign affairs, Brugha defense, Stack home affairs, Collins finances, Barton economic affairs, and Cosgrave local government. With De Valera included, that put seven men in charge of deciding government policies, some moderate nationalists and others firm Republicans, all drawn together under De Valera's leadership in seeking Ireland's recognition as a nation. But now, while Ireland was enjoying a summer of peace under the truce, the threat of renewed war hung in the balance, and for each man there were crucial personal decisions as to what was best for the Irish people.

De Valera spoke to the Dail about future relations with Britain and publicly hinted at a plan he had been working on privately but had not yet completed. Ireland could not accept a simple political combination "with the enemy that has despoiled us most," he said, but there could be "relations which would bring us more closely together for mutual interest." He hoped for "an association that would be consistent with our right to see that we were the judges of what was in our own interest, and that we were not compelled to leave the judgment of what were our own interests . . . to others."

When he fully developed it, this was to become the key to De Valera's attitude toward the British for years to come. It was to be his plan for "External Association," an Ireland free of King and Crown in making its own democratic decisions on all matters within the country, but willing to be associated with Britain in affairs outside the country, in such things as treaties and trade agreements. Internally an independent Ireland with the sovereignty of the people supreme; externally a Commonwealth partner to the extent of sharing mutual interests with England in areas of benefit to both.

Meanwhile De Valera and Lloyd George were exchanging letters and telegrams. Fifteen messages went back and forth in what amounted to a detailed public debate over resuming negotiations, with both men verbally sparring for advantage. De Valera officially refused the British terms, partition and a limited Dominion, insisted that the Irish people alone had the right to determine their government, and said that Irish envoys could join in a conference only as representatives of an independent sovereign state.

Lloyd George refused to discuss any settlement which would take Ireland outside the British Commonwealth, said that to meet the Irish representatives on such grounds would be an act of disloyalty to the King, and argued that "government by the consent of the governed" meant free equality as a loyal Dominion, not the right to establish an Irish Republic or to secede from the Empire. He was, however, willing to meet Irish representatives to examine how "the association of Ireland with the Community of Nations known as the British Empire may best be reconciled with Irish national aspirations."

De Valera, anxious to present his plan for External Association, found a solution that would allow for a conference without backing down on the claim that the Irish could enter it only as representatives of a sovereign independent state. They would not insist in advance that the English recognize them as such, but would hope for a conference that would be "free and without prejudice." It was a happy phrase and Lloyd George promptly adopted it in issuing an invitation to a conference to start October 11, 1921. De Valera accepted, with the understanding that by coming into conference neither side was in any way committed to accepting the position of the other.

Everybody, including Lloyd George, assumed that De Valera would head the Irish delegation. But that was not De Valera's strategy. When his cabinet of seven met in Dublin to choose delegates to the London conference De Valera surprised them by saying he preferred to remain at home.

As head of state, he explained, his proper place was in Dublin where he could handle any crisis that might develop if the talks had to be broken off, and if they came to a temporary deadlock he could use his influence from outside to get them started again. Delegates could refer questions to him, claim the need for consultation with the government, and gain delays and advantages in bargaining. In Dublin he would be in a better position to keep the Irish people united in their understanding of what was being fought for at London.

He felt that his influence would be greater if he could speak freely and independently as President rather than as one of the delegates. If America's President Wilson had remained in Washington at the end of the World War to guide the Congress and people of the United States instead of personally heading the American delegation to France, De Valera pointed out, he might have gained more than at Versailles.

De Valera had his way but his cabinet split four to three in voting on it, with Griffith, Collins and Cosgrave a minority who thought he should head the delegation. He then proposed that Griffith should head it, with Collins second in command. Collins at first refused, saying he had little understanding of international politics, but after much persuasion he reluctantly consented. Barton, as an economics expert, and Eamonn Duggan and Gavan Duffy as lawyers, finally were chosen to round out the Irish delegation. Erskine Childers was named Secretary, over Griffith's strong objections.

Doubts, differences and clashes of personality were to go with the Irish delegation, to be exploited by Lloyd George. De Valera's reasoning was good, but the consequences proved tragic. Irishmen have never yet stopped arguing over whether he should have gone to London or stayed home.

CHAPTER 11

President De Valera sent the Irish delegates off to London as "Envoys Plenipotentiary from the elected Government of the Republic of Ireland," which was another way of telling the British that they came demanding recognition of the Republic. But they took with them a confidential rough outline of his plan for External Association, which he hoped would give Ireland complete freedom within its borders and at the same time would reassure the British and let them save face.

He wanted the Irish delegates to argue that Britain should give up all claim to govern or legislate for Ireland and that it should recognize the Irish Republic as a sovereign state in which no vestige of British authority was to remain. But the British could keep limited control over Irish foreign policy and would not have to admit that they had been forced by armed rebellion to allow the Irish to sever all connections with the Empire. As an "External Associate," Ireland would become an equal partner of the Commonwealth states in matters of vital Empire concern.

The delegates were given full power to "negotiate and con-

clude on behalf of Ireland . . . a treaty or treaties of settlement,"
but they had explicit written instructions that before they
agreed to any major decisions or signed a final treaty they
would refer them to De Valera's government in Dublin and
await a reply.

De Valera warned the Irish people not to get their hopes too
high. "The only peace that . . . can end this struggle will be a
peace . . . guaranteeing a freedom worthy of the sufferings
endured to secure it," he said. "Such a peace will not be easy
to obtain. . . . The delegates, therefore, indulge in no foolish
hopes, nor should the country indulge in them. The peace that
will end this conflict will be secured . . . by the stern determination of a close-knit nation steeled to the acceptance of death
rather than abandonment of its rightful liberty."

But there were high hopes in Ireland because of the truce
and to many the prospect of a treaty that would ensure peace
was more important than the terms of that treaty. When the
Irish delegates arrived in London, there was a great outpouring
of the British people to welcome them. Peace was in the air,
public opinion was demanding an end to the troubles in Ireland, and both sides were pressed to reach some reasonable
settlement.

Across the conference table from the Irish delegates, the
British arrayed imposing statesmen. None was more skilled in
bending other men to his will than Lloyd George himself. With
him, among others, were the great British Parliamentarian,
Austen Chamberlain; the famed lawyer and debater, Lord
Birkenhead; and not least of all, Winston Churchill, the orator
of British Imperialism.

Griffith, Collins and the other delegates fought hard to get
the British to accept De Valera's plan of External Association,
but the British held to their own offer of Dominion status.
There was some give and take at first on comparatively minor

issues, but real trouble came over the two major questions of the partition of Ulster and Irish allegiance to the Crown. Lloyd George skillfully played one issue against the other to break the Irish delegation.

De Valera had held together a government that embraced all degrees of nationalism. He had preserved harmony by his ingenious ability to adapt and modify details without losing sight of what were to him the basic principles of Irish freedom. His External Association plan had been conceived not only as a bridge between Ireland and England but as one upon which he hoped all sections of the nationalist movement could stand.

The difference between being a Dominion of the British Empire and being a Republic associated with the Empire was far more to De Valera than one of mere words. It was the difference between Ireland's right to choose its own government or to surrender to a government imposed upon it. He never considered for a moment allowing the King of England to remain the King of Ireland, even though the same monarch might be the King of the Commonwealth with which Ireland would associate from the outside. Among the cabinet members who stayed in Dublin with him, Brugha and Stack were extreme in their Republican views. Cosgrave considered the difference between External Association and Dominion status important but not fundamental.

Arthur Griffith, as head of the delegation to London, soon found himself in a personally agonizing position. He had long ago recommended a dual monarchy, with the King of England also ruling as King of Ireland over a separate Irish Kingdom and parliament. Griffith had watched his Sinn Fein outgrow his own moderate nationalism to become the political party of the Republic and he had supported the Republic as the rallying force of the Irish people but with personal reservations. He was not a passionate Republican, not to the extent of persisting in the demand for a Republic at the cost of renewed war. But now he had to argue for External Association, which was De Valera's plan, not his, and De Valera was far away in Dublin.

Michael Collins, second in command of the delegation, loved the Republic. Few men in Ireland had fought more valiantly for its cause. But he was essentially a practical man, more interested in results than in the abstractions of politics. Collins was not one to draw a life and death distinction between forms of government. With war suspended he wanted Ireland freed of British occupation and controls. If association with the Empire in one way or another had been decided upon, then he wanted to get on with practical matters such as trade and defense agreements and wished the political settlements could be left to others.

The London conference had been underway only thirteen days when Lloyd George announced that he and Winston Churchill would like to meet Griffith and Collins in private. They agreed to the meeting and from then on the whole character of the negotiations changed. The Irish delegation never sat in the conference room as a unit again. In the weeks that followed, Lloyd George invited Griffith, Collins or other delegates to private meetings and went to work to win them over with all the mastery he had shown at Versailles. The talks became an ordeal for the Irish delegates of testing their official arguments against their personal convictions.

What Lloyd George held out to Griffith and Collins was what they wanted most, the hope of a united land returning to ways of peace, with British troops immediately withdrawn. He held out the possibility of an unpartitioned Ireland, with Ulster included in an All-Ireland Parliament, if they would help convince the Ulstermen to come into it by agreeing that Ireland should be a British Dominion. If Ulster refused, Lloyd George suggested there might be a boundary commission which perhaps would give the South two or more of Ulster's six counties, so that Ulster would decide it had to join the rest of Ireland in one Dominion.

Griffith and Collins, drawn closer in their views of what was best for Ireland and gradually divided from the rest of the delegation, continued to hold out for External Association, but against a Dominion status that Lloyd George made increasingly attractive. Behind the British proposals was always the threat that any rejection of them would bring upon Ireland a war more terrible than any it had known, at a horrible cost of Irish lives and national ruin.

But to De Valera, Brugha and Stack in Dublin the cost of Dominion was freedom itself. De Valera and the delegates exchanged frequent messages and between talks the delegates came to Dublin regularly to consult with him. He sensed the dangers of a division and tried to keep unity. Speaking about the delegates at the convention of Sinn Fein that reelected him its president at the end of October, De Valera said: "What may happen, I am not able to judge, but I am anxious that you should realize the difficulties. . . . As sure as the nation is divided, the nation will be tricked."

By late November, 1921, the British had rejected the Irish proposals, but Griffith and Collins had fought for and won British agreement to put Ireland on the same Dominion status as Canada. The British presented their written terms for a treaty on December 1. Ireland was offered a British Dominion to be called the "Irish Free State," with generally the same laws and constitution as Canada and with an Irish parliament and an executive responsible to that parliament. However there would be a British Governor-General appointed by the King and members of the Irish parliament would have to take an oath that was worded:

"I . . . do solemnly swear true faith and allegiance to the Constitution of the Irish Free State . . . and that I will be faithful to His Majesty King George V, his heirs and successors . . . in virtue of the common citizenship of Ireland with Great Britain and her adherence to and membership of the group of nations forming the British Commonwealth of Nations."

Northern Ireland, if it so voted, could refuse to come into the All-Ireland Parliament, in which case Ulster would keep its own separate government and parliament. If the North did decide to stay out of the Free State a commission would be set up to consider new boundary lines for Ulster.

The Irish delegates hurried to Dublin for a full meeting of De Valera's cabinet. For seven hours they argued over whether or not to accept the British terms. Griffith and Collins thought rejecting the treaty would plunge Ireland into war. De Valera and those who sided with him said the treaty could never be accepted as it stood.

De Valera would not subscribe to the oath of allegiance to an English King or to a document that gave Ulster the power to vote itself out of an Irish state. He said it guaranteed neither independence nor an unpartitioned Ireland, "neither this nor that."

Griffith argued that nothing more could be wrung from the British. He held that the treaty practically recognized the Republic, put allegiance to Ireland first, and called for nothing from the Irish people that they would be willing to go to war about. Rejection would give Ulster the excuse it wanted to keep Ireland divided, Griffith believed, but a signed treaty would create a united Ireland. He wanted the delegates to sign the treaty and then leave it up to the Dail to decide whether to approve what they had done.

Collins, although against the oath, feared that rejecting the treaty might be a gamble that could bring war in a week.

Delegate Duggan also thought the treaty should be signed, but delegates Barton and Duffy thought the British were bluffing and were against signing. Among the cabinet members, Brugha and Stack were totally opposed to the treaty.

De Valera believed there was still a good chance to get the British to modify their terms. As a concession, the Irish might agree to some sort of an oath that would recognize the King as head of an External Association, he said, "if we get all else we want." He was anxious to have the delegates go back and secure peace on "honorable terms" if possible, but by making the British understand the Irish were willing to go to war if necessary to insure Ireland's unity and internal freedom.

Griffith refused to take responsibility for breaking off negotiations over an oath to the King if that meant war. He would argue for all the concessions he could get, but if it came to a breaking point he would accept the treaty and then put it before the people.

Faced with Griffith's refusal, De Valera considered changing the delegation and going to London at the head of it himself. But a cabinet majority finally turned down the proposed treaty and sent Griffith and the delegates back to London to argue again for External Association. If it came to a showdown, Griffith was to tell Lloyd George the document could not be signed and that it had become a matter for the Dail to decide. In that case, Griffith promised to bring an unsigned treaty back to submit to the Dail, where he intended to recommend its approval.

Assured by Griffith's promise that nothing would be signed in London unless Dublin agreed, De Valera gave up the idea of going himself. But it was a badly divided Irish delegation that returned to London for a meeting at 10 Downing Street with Lloyd George and some of his ministers on Sunday evening, December 4. Collins refused to accompany the other delegates to the meeting. Griffith and Duggan went reluctantly, only to preserve the delegation's outward unity. Yet Griffith, despite his own feelings in favor of the treaty, argued External Association for two hours with Lloyd George.

The British accused the Irish of going back to a position that would end Ireland's chance to become a willing member of the Empire and that would bring all negotiations to an end. Lloyd George and his ministers finally got to their feet and announced that the meeting was over. The crisis, the Prime Minister said, would be put before the King and the British cabinet the next day. War against Ireland had become more than an indefinite threat.

Before Lloyd George saw the King, however, he arranged for a private talk Monday morning with Collins, who agreed to it after much urging by Griffith. Lloyd George convinced Collins the situation could be saved only by another conference that afternoon. Late in the day, Collins and Griffith talked Barton into going with them to confront Lloyd George, Lord Birkenhead, Austen Chamberlain and Winston Churchill. Griffith and Collins sought and got some fresh concessions from the British. But the British ministers, as Churchill later wrote, were "unutterably wearied" by "two months of futilities and rigamarole," and the Irish delegation were "in actual desperation . . . knowing well that death stood at their elbows."

Lloyd George delivered a blunt ultimatum. The Irish delegates must settle now. They must sign the agreement for a treaty. The British would "concede no more and debate no further." Sign immediately, he said, or immediately face war. He pointed out that the delegates had been fully empowered by the Dublin government to make a settlement and that it now was upon them to do so with no further instructions from Dublin. They could take no unsigned treaty away with them. Either they would sign it that day or the full military force of the Empire would be turned against Ireland.

Griffith needed no ultimatum to convince him the treaty settlement offered Ireland as much as he thought it could hope for from Britain. After seven hundred years, British occupation was to cease. Ireland was to be a "Free State," in his view a republic in everything but name, with its own parliament and a Dominion status far more generous that he and other leaders had dared dream was possible only a few years before. It would, as Griffith was to put it, "give Ireland control of her own destinies . . . put the future in our own hands—enable us to stand on our own feet, develop our own civilization . . . lay the foundation of peace and friendship . . . end the conflict of centuries."

He had been in favor of it before he returned from Dublin and the cabinet showdown with De Valera. If he had promised to bring back an unsigned treaty to put before the Dail he also had made it clear that he would not choose war over an oath of allegiance to the King. Faced now with the British ultimatum, Griffith chose peace and the settlement he believed offered promise for Ireland's future.

"I will give the answer of the Irish delegation tonight," Griffith told Lloyd George, "but as for myself, I will personally sign this agreement and recommend it to my countrymen." Even if every other delegate refused, Griffith said, "I will sign."

That was not enough, Lloyd George answered. "Every delegate must sign the document and undertake to recommend it," he said, and responsibility for war would rest upon any delegate who refused. "You can have until ten p.m. tonight," he told them, "to decide whether you will give peace or war to your country."

It was after seven when the Irish withdrew and went to the Hans Place house that was the delegation's London headquarters. Griffith, Collins and Barton were joined there by Duggan and Duffy for the decision they had only a few hours to make. For each, the signing had become an individual decision, and nobody telephoned to Dublin or De Valera for instructions. Griffith strongly urged them to sign. Duggan sided with him. Collins had decided the settlement was all that could be obtained, that the Republic's Army was in no position to continue a successful war against the British, and that the treaty offered a "stepping stone" to greater eventual freedoms.

Barton and Duffy refused to sign. The other three declared they would go back alone and sign and they put on their coats to leave. Long after ten Barton finally gave in to the argument that the treaty, even if signed, still would have to be put before the Dail for final approval and that his signing would give the people themselves a chance to decide whether there was to be war. Duffy could not stand alone and take sole responsibility for war. He at last agreed to give his signature "under duress."

It was close to midnight when the Irish delegates returned to 10 Downing Street and after two o'clock on the morning of December 6, 1921, before they and the British signed the articles of agreement. During all the weeks of conferences the British and the Irish had never shaken hands, the enmity had been too bitter, but now Lloyd George and the British ministers stood and walked around the table to offer their hands. "We had become allies and associates in a common cause," Churchill wrote, "the cause of the Irish Treaty and of peace between two races and two islands."

The Irish delegates would bring home both a treaty and an ultimatum. Arthur Griffith would see them as men who "have brought back the flag" and a "treaty of equality." President De Valera would see them as delegates who had violated their promises, acted without consulting the Dublin government, brought back an oath to the King of England, a treaty that fixed the partition of the six counties of Ulster from the rest of Ireland, men who had turned their backs on the Republic.

He had received no message from them. He had no knowledge that the agreement had been signed until he read about it in the morning newspapers, which gave no details. When he saw the first headlines he hoped, as unlikely as it seemed, that the British had agreed to External Association, since the cabinet had sent the delegates back to London to accept nothing less.

De Valera learned the truth that night. Delegate Duggan arrived from London and handed him an envelope containing the agreement and told him it would be published within the hour in both Dublin and London. "Whether I have seen it or not?" De Valera asked. "Whether I approve it or not?" Duggan answered, "That is what was arranged."

By telegram De Valera summoned the absent members of his cabinet from London. A full cabinet meeting, he announced, would be held at noon December 8, to decide what was to be done about "the proposed treaty with Great Britain." Some Republican Army commanders wanted to arrest the delegates for "high treason" as soon as they set foot in Ireland but De Valera and Brugha refused to allow that.

When the cabinet met, De Valera tried for five hours to persuade them not to recommend the treaty to the Dail. Cosgrave, at first undecided, was won over to Griffith's view that a Free State Dominion offered peace and a chance to establish a recognized Irish government. Finally a vote was taken. De Valera lost. By four to three—Griffith, Collins, Barton and Cosgrave against De Valera, Brugha and Stack—the cabinet recommended acceptance.

The break had come. The Republican government that De Valera had for so long held together, despite extremes of political viewpoints within it, had split apart. "I cannot recommend acceptance of this treaty either to Dail Eireann or to the country," he said in a public proclamation that evening. "The terms . . . are in violent conflict with the wishes of the majority of this nation as expressed freely in successive elections during the past three years."

He announced the Dail would meet the following Wednesday. "I ask the people to maintain during the interval the same discipline as heretofore," he said, pleading for national calm and tolerance. "The greatest test of our people has come. Let us face it worthily, without bitterness and above all without recriminations. There is a definite constitutional way of resolving our political differences—let us not depart from it."

But the Irish people already were dividing, for or against the treaty, for the Free State or for the Republic. More dangerously, the Irish Army also was dividing. De Valera, and Griffith and Collins on the other side, all tried for constitutional settlement, until emotion turned men with guns to shooting each other and leadership was lost to force.

CHAPTER **12**

President De Valera pleaded with the Dail not to destroy the Republic by accepting the treaty. The fact that it had been signed by the Irish delegates weighed heavily against him, but if he could get the Dail to reject it he hoped the British would be forced to reopen negotiations.

By coincidence, debate over the treaty began the same day, December 14, 1921, in both the Parliament in London and the Dail in Dublin. The British Parliament ratified it within forty-eight hours. In the Dail, the emotion-charged debate went on for weeks. Arguing that the treaty was "a thing which will not even reconcile our own people," De Valera said, "I am against this treaty, not because I am a man of war, but a man of peace."

Many saw promise for peace in accepting the treaty. Some joyously hailed it as an Irish victory; others were merely resigned to it. Weary of fighting, they welcomed peace at any price, and to the majority the price at first seemed small. The threat to peace De Valera feared was not only from the British but from the division of the Irish people.

Just as his own cabinet had been, the Dail was split in two

by the issue. The newspapers, big business, church leaders, and a strong group of nationalists all favored the treaty. Arthur Griffith, whose loyalty to Ireland few would question, and Michael Collins, the patriot hero, had not only put their names to it but now led the battle for it in the Dail.

De Valera had been working on a new draft of his plan for External Association, worded to offend English prejudices as little as possible, but still to preserve the Republic. The day would come, long in the future, when External Association would be the accepted relationship of the Commonwealth Nations to the British Empire, but now it was ahead of its time. Pro-treaty forces in the Dail wanted to hear no new version of it. They had no intention of tearing up the signed treaty to submit a compromise for fresh negotiations.

On January 7, 1922, the treaty finally came to a vote. In three minutes, it was over. The Dail approved the treaty by a margin of seven votes, 64 to 57. De Valera and the Republicans had lost.

There was an angry commotion in the Dail when the vote was announced and he pleaded for order. "We have had four years of magnificent discipline in our nation. The world is looking at us now—" His voice broke. He was unable to go on. He sat down, with tears in his eyes, and put his hands to his face.

Two days later he issued a direct challenge in the Dail by announcing his resignation as President. If the Dail wanted to reelect him, it would do so knowing that he stood "definitely for the Irish Republic as it was established . . . and I will stand by no policy whatever that is not consistent with that." He knew that many of the deputies who had voted for the treaty would not want to vote against him personally. His reelection, if his backers could win it, would have the effect of nullifying the treaty vote.

Collins quickly said that "no one here in this assembly or in Ireland wants to be in the position of opposing President De Valera," and suggested that he remain as President, with a committee formed from both sides to carry on the functions of government while the treaty terms were carried out. Griffith also said there was "no need for him to resign. . . . We want him with us."

De Valera refused to remain President in name only. He pointed out that constitutionally the Republic could be disestablished only by the direct vote of the Irish people and that until there was an election the Dail would remain the supreme government. If he were chosen again as President, his government would stand by the Republic, and would be responsible only to the Dail.

He came within two votes of carrying it off. No other candidate was put up against him. Fifty-eight deputies voted for the motion to reelect him, but sixty voted against him, and De Valera no longer was President of the Irish Republic.

When Griffith was put up for President the next day, there was an uproar. De Valera and his followers charged it was illegal and unconstitutional to use the Dail to elect a President supposedly sworn to uphold the Republic who at the same time meant to create a Provisional Free State Government. That would be putting Griffith in the position of having "with the right hand to maintain the Republic and with the left to knock it down," De Valera said. "No matter what Mr. Griffith says or undertakes to do, every Republican in the country will be suspicious of every act he is taking. . . . It does not conduce to the maintenance of order. . . . It is not in the best interests of the country . . ."

He and his supporters rose and walked out of the Dail in protest, refusing to have any part in the vote. In their absence, the remaining half of the deputies elected Griffith to head a

new administration. Having made his protest, Ex-President
De Valera led his men back in and promised that the Republicans would not stand in Griffith's way while he was acting in
his capacity as President of the Republic, but that when
Griffith acted in his other capacity as head of a Provisional
Free State government "we will have to insist and continue
insisting . . . that that government is not the legitimate government of this country."

The Dail continued to function as the parliament of the
Republic, with both sides pledged to respect its authority, but
meanwhile the half of the Dail's members who were led by
Griffith met as a British Parliament of Southern Ireland on
January 14, 1922, under the terms of the treaty, and elected
a Provisional Government as a required first step toward creating an Irish Free State Dominion. Collins was chosen the
Provisional Government's chairman, to avoid putting Griffith
in the position of being officially chief executive of both the
Provisional Government and the Dail. Two days later, Collins
and his new ministers went to Dublin Castle to take over the
administration of Southern Ireland from Great Britain. The
British, who had agreed to evacuate their troops, began to turn
over major military barracks to the Irish.

But the treaty provided that during the one-year period
before the Provisional Government could become a Free State
it had to be approved by direct vote of the people of Ireland.
Winston Churchill, as Britain's Colonial Secretary, summoned
Collins to London and advised an election as soon as possible,
within a few months. De Valera was determined to delay the
election for as long as possible. Time, he was convinced, would
be on his side. The people needed time to understand the full
implications of the treaty, time to realize they were losing the
Republic they had given their blood to establish and that they
were not only keeping the King in rule but were giving up the

North of Ireland to partition, time to recover from their weariness and reaffirm their courage, to reject the Provisional Government so that it would die with the Free State still unborn.

Irish government was caught in a maze. De Valera held no official office, but remained leader of the Republicans. Griffith was President of the Republic, but leader of the Free State forces. His interim authority came from the Dail, but he had been elected by only half the Dail, with the other half protesting that was unconstitutional. His half of the Dail had created a Provisional Free State government. De Valera's half of the Dail refused to recognize the legality of the Provisional Government.

The Provisional Government, while supposedly under control of the Dail, made decisions of its own. But the Dail and the Republic remained supreme unless abolished by a vote of the people. Britain had never legally recognized the Dail or the Republic, but it had signed a treaty with envoys of the Republic, by which it recognized the Provisional Government pending its acceptance by the voters. Meanwhile Britain officially still ruled Ireland under British law, part of which provided the separate Parliament of Northern Ireland, which the Republic did not recognize.

On paper, Ireland had at least half a dozen bodies of government; in practice, Southern Ireland operated under conflicting double authority of the Dail and the Provisional Government. It was a system that set Ireland dangerously adrift. Authority was where each individual sought to find it, according to his own political beliefs. The result was near-anarchy and some men again began to put their faith in guns instead of government.

What had been the Irish Republican Army was growing into two armies. Brigades and divisions were lining up in opposing ranks for the Provisional Free State Government or the Republic. Soldiers who found themselves in a unit that didn't suit their political views would quit and join another that did. Entire commands became almost solidly pro-treaty or anti-treaty. As the British withdrew troops, leaving the Irish to quarrel among themselves over which military force should replace them, there were armed clashes.

De Valera, during debates in the Dail, had made a particular point of obtaining a pledge that the Dail and not the Provisional Government would keep control of the Army. Griffith's new Minister of Defense, Army Chief of Staff Richard Mulcahy, had pledged that "the Army will remain the Army of the Irish Republic." Outwardly, the whole Army maintained allegiance to the Dail, but like Mulcahy, the majority of the Army's Headquarters' staff favored the treaty.

When some of the officers at Army Headquarters began to act as if the Army were a military branch of the Provisional Government, whole divisions openly broke away, declared themselves independent forces, and refused to take further orders from Headquarters. Griffith, as President, used the Dail to try to prohibit a meeting of Army commanders under threat of arrest. But top officers who favored the Republic defied the order, held a meeting, and established a Republican command that would answer to no government at all.

As Volunteers they pledged themselves to ignore both the Provisional Government and the Dail and to be responsible only to the Irish people for preservation of the Republic. Rory O'Connor, one of the leading officers and a veteran of the Revolution who had been wounded in the Easter Rising, claimed to speak for eighty per cent of the Army when he told reporters, "The Volunteers are not going into the British Empire. They stand for Irish liberty."

De Valera had appealed to the Army to obey the existing Headquarters and the Dail, but O'Connor said, "The Army for which I speak cannot." O'Connor accused Chief of Staff

Mulcahy of having broken his pledge to De Valera to maintain an Army of the Republic, and of having instead tried to create a Free State Army. Griffith, he charged, had violated his oath as President of the Dail. O'Connor declared that the new army of Volunteers, tied to no government or political party, would issue its own orders "all over the country."

The Republican Volunteers called themselves the "Irish Republican Army," although the old army of that name was now as divided as the country itself, with pro-treaty officers and men loyal to Chief of Staff Mulcahy supporting the Provisional Government. De Valera, with the Volunteers beyond his control and defying the Dail, faced the dilemma of wanting to arouse the very spirit and courage they represented in resisting the treaty, yet also wanting to preserve constitutional government.

Certainly he did not seek civil war, any more than Griffith or any responsible Irish leader sought that. "Let there be no talk of fratricidal strife," De Valera had said in the Dail. "That is all nonsense." But while reviewing troops of Volunteers, he warned that unless the treaty were rejected and the unity of the Republic restored "then these men, in order to achieve freedom, will have to march over the dead bodies of their own brothers. They will have to wade through Irish blood."

✄ ✄

CHAPTER 13

The British, as they always had been, were the real
enemy to Ireland's freedom to De Valera. He saw the British
Government directly dictating the policies and decisions of the
Provisional Government to undermine the Republic and the
Dail.

Collins and Griffith were being summoned regularly to
London, to be told by Churchill exactly what Britain would
and would not accept. And Churchill was declaring that "we
have said again and again that we will not in any circumstances
tolerate . . . an independent Republic or a Republican form of
government in Ireland."

Both sides in Ireland had agreed to acknowledge the
sovereignty of the Dail, but in practical fact the Provisional
Government controlled the purse strings, and the purse was
Britain's. The British were financing the Provisional Government while the Dail had no money for any of its departments.
Britain was arming the Provisional Government's forces with
guns and ammunition, paying for its soldiers, keeping British
artillery handy, maintaining British force in Irish treaty ports,

holding armed divisions threateningly poised above the border of Northern Ireland.

"The British Government," De Valera said in an interview, "prevents the Irish people's free choice. . . . The threat of war from this government is intimidation operating on the side of Mr. Griffith and Mr. Collins as sure and as definite as if these gentlemen were using it themselves."

De Valera was still president of Sinn Fein, the controlling organization to which nationalists on both sides of the treaty dispute belonged, and when its three thousand delegates from all over the country met in Dublin, he asked them "in God's name not to give a British monarch a democratic title in Ireland." He appealed to Sinn Fein to refuse its support to any candidate who was for the treaty.

The convention seemed likely to do just that, so Griffith made an agreement with De Valera "to avoid a division of the Sinn Fein organization and to avert the danger to the country of an immediate election." Under the compromise, Griffith's side avoided having Sinn Fein declare itself against the treaty, and De Valera won a delay in the national elections from April to June.

The Irish Republican Volunteers took matters into their own hands on the night of April 13, 1922. Dublin brigades, led by Rory O'Connor, occupied the Four Courts, the great law buildings that were the center of the judicial system. They entered quietly, without opposition, barricaded windows with sacks filled with clay, and turned the enclosed buildings and courtyard into a Republican Army headquarters at the heart of the city. A number of other Dublin buildings also were occupied. From the Four Courts, the Republican officers began to direct military operations in various parts of Ireland.

O'Connor denied that it was a second Revolution; it was not a revolt against the government, but a declaration by force that there was no government, and a challenge by the Republican Army to take over the country by military rule unless its conditions were met by the Dail. In a letter to each member of the Dail, the Republican Volunteers warned they were giving the Dail "an opportunity, probably the last . . . of saving the country from civil war, now threatened by those who have abandoned the Republic."

Aside from acknowledging that it had received the letter, the Dail, under Griffith's Presidency, took no action. The Provisional Government, on its part, made no immediate attempt to drive the Republican Army out of its new headquarters in the Four Courts. Nobody really wanted to start a civil war. Griffith did not want to be the one to "strike the first blow." Collins thought the split in Army forces somehow could be repaired. De Valera hoped some political settlement could be reached.

He sympathized with the Republican Army's motives, if not with its acts. "If the Irish people were allowed a free choice," he said, "they would choose by an overwhelming majority exactly what these armed forces desire." But De Valera had no control over the Army or its actions he told a *Chicago Tribune* correspondent. "It has now definitely reverted to its former independent status."

On the very day that O'Connor and the Republican Army took over the Four Courts, De Valera and Brugha had gone to confer with Griffith and Collins in an effort by all of them to avert civil war. Dublin's Archbishop Walsh and Lord Mayor O'Neill brought the two parties together. Labor attempted to mediate. Army officers on both sides tried to reach their own agreement.

The conferences broke down in arguments over the coming election. Griffith and Collins insisted that the people had to decide in June whether or not they would accept the treaty;

De Valera and Brugha held that the immediate concern was peace and that the treaty issue should be postponed while an interim government was elected to restore single authority and normal conditions.

That would give time, De Valera said, "for the present passions to subside . . . and the fundamental differences between the two sides to be appreciated," and time to revise the antiquated voting lists so that thousands of younger voters would not be denied the ballot. He hoped that the Army could be reunited under a single command and that the proposed constitution of the Free State could be introduced so citizens could study it before they voted. A vote taken immediately, he warned, would be repudiated by militant Republicans. No election could decide the issue of Free State versus Republic unless there was "peace and order" so that people would accept a democratic decision.

Privately, De Valera and Collins continued their talks, both aware that if they failed civil war was almost inevitable. Time and again they broke off the discussions, unable to overcome their differences, but driven by a shared anxiety to reach some agreement. After almost a month, they signed a pact, which was announced to a cheering Dail. The threat of civil war, it seemed, might be over.

De Valera and Collins had worked out a plan for a National Coalition Government in which the two sides would have a single combined administration. Under the agreement each side would put up candidates for the coming election who would then all run together as a national panel under the common party banner of Sinn Fein. Locally voters would be choosing individual candidates, but nationally they would be electing an agreed-upon membership in a new Irish legislature, no matter whether the Sinn Feiner who won top position in any particular election district was for or against the treaty.

So each side would keep its present strength, the Free State party would choose sixty-six of the combined Sinn Fein candidates and the Republicans fifty-eight. Other political parties might oppose the Sinn Fein candidates, but under Ireland's system of proportional representation Sinn Fein expected to win enough votes spread over the whole panel to elect it. After the panel was elected, the new administration would be appointed according to previous agreement. A combined Army then would elect its own Minister of Defense.

Although the votes might indicate preferences for or against the treaty, the people would not be forced to choose at once between a government committed to the Empire or a government pledged to keep the Republic at the risk of war. Whatever stand the representatives who were elected took on the treaty, the voters still would keep a Sinn Fein Coalition Government in which both sides would have a choice in preserving peace. At some indefinite future time, when things had calmed down and all issues were understood, the treaty itself could be put directly to a vote in a general election.

De Valera told the Dail that the plan was not a triumph for one section or the other, but a great triumph for the Irish nation. Collins said it would bring stable conditions to the country that would enable it to face whatever changes were to come. Such was the hope, and it appeared at first that the plan might work. De Valera and Collins issued joint appeals to the voters to support the combined candidates and to reduce election contests to a minimum. In the early stages of the campaign the two spoke from the same platforms together, apparently happy to be comrades again, whatever differences they had over the treaty.

But from the moment news of the pact reached London, the British government was furious. The British immediately halted their withdrawal of troops from Ireland, ordered fresh troops to strengthen their forces in the North, and suspended supplies of guns and ammunition to the Provisional Government. The treaty would be considered broken, they warned, if Republicans were allowed to become part of an Irish government without taking the oath of allegiance and signing a declaration of adherence to the treaty for a Free State.

Ulster's Unionists and their supporters in London saw the pact as a threat to the North. Sir Henry Wilson, who as chief of Britain's military staff had constantly urged the British to crush Sinn Fein and to keep Ireland united with England, called the election agreement "the surrender of the Provisional Government to De Valera" and said "the Union must be reestablished."

Churchill called Collins and Griffith to London, denounced the election plan, and warned of the "gravity of the breach." He noted that Griffith was not in sympathy with what had been done, but that Collins was "half defiant, half obviously embarrassed." In answer to questions in the House of Commons, Churchill said publicly that the British troops in Dublin "are remaining in the position they hold." In the event of "a setting up of a Republic," he said, "it would be the intention of the (British) government to hold Dublin as one of the preliminary and essential steps for the military operations."

Collins and Griffith sat in the visitors' gallery during the House of Commons debate, and heard not only Churchill's warning, but Sir Henry Wilson's repeated threat that British troops from the North might be ordered across the border into Southern Ireland "if serious trouble arises on the frontier."

Under the renewed threat of possible war by England, the Irish people carried on their election campaign. An increased number of independent candidates and others opposed to Sinn Fein entered the race, which threatened to wreck the Coalition. Campaigning was violent in places, with speakers shot at and gun-battles between those for and against the treaty. Republicans objected when the proclamation for the election was issued in the name of the Provisional Government instead of the Dail.

Griffith, in London, was having troubles with the British over the proposed new Free State constitution. Lloyd George called the first draft presented by an Irish committee an outrage, and took up a pencil to strike out parts he said Britain would not permit. The Irish people were not to see it before election day.

Collins, in Ireland, became increasingly worried by the menacing statements from London. He finally made an election speech in Cork that Republicans took to be a breaking of his pact with De Valera. He warned of the "very serious situation" the country was facing and appealed to citizens, in effect, to forget the Coalition and "to vote for the candidates you think best."

To Republicans that was a direct bid for treaty votes, a violation of the terms of the election. In Dublin newspaper headlines spread the word that Collins was asking the country's voters to back Free State Government instead of a Coalition Government. London newspapers reported that the Irish election had been thrown wide open.

When the returns of the June 16 election were counted they produced results that could be interpreted two ways. Sinn Fein won a clear majority, 94 seats out of 128, and on that basis the decision could be considered a mandate for Coalition government. But among the elected Sinn Fein deputies, 58 were for the treaty and only 36 were against, and on that basis it could be considered a mandate for a Free State.

The British considered a new Irish parliament elected. Under the terms of the new constitution, however, no Republicans elected to it could sit as members unless they took the compulsory oath of allegiance to the King, which they would not take. By the time the new Dail was due to meet, Coalition

Government had become impossible. Political solution had failed.

Six days after the election, on June 22, British military commander Sir Henry Wilson, hated by the Irish perhaps more than any other man, was shot to death on the steps of his London home. For years he had been against all peaceful dealings with Irish nationalists, had advocated the harshest military action, and in particular was held responsible by the Irish for the persecution of Catholics in Ulster.

His two assassins made no attempt to escape. Both were Irishmen, and both also were British Army veterans who had fought in France, where one of them had lost a leg in action against the Germans. They freely admitted "supporting the aspirations of our fellow countrymen" for the same reason they had fought in Europe, "for the rights of small nationalities." Quickly tried and sentenced to be executed, one of them, Reginald Dunne, declared, "You can condemn us to death today, but you cannot deprive us of the belief that what we have done was necessary to preserve the lives and happiness of our countrymen in Ireland."

There was no direct evidence to connect them with the Irish Republican Army. In fact there were unproved rumors that Michael Collins secretly had given orders for Sir Henry Wilson's "execution." Perhaps the assassins simply acted on their own. In Ireland as a whole there was little weeping over Wilson's death. Asked by reporters for a statement, De Valera said, "The killing of a human being is an awful act, but as awful when the victim is the humble worker or peasant as when the victim is placed in the seats of the mighty. I do not know who they were who shot Sir Henry Wilson or why they shot him. . . . I do not approve but I must not pretend to misunderstand."

Britain, seething with horror and outrage over the assassination, blamed the Four Courts' garrison for the killing. Even before Wilson was shot to death Churchill had been demanding that Collins must oust the Republican Army from the Four Courts by force, but Collins, hoping to the last for some political settlement, had hesitated.

Churchill now issued a public warning in a speech in the House of Commons that "if through weakness, want of courage, or some other less creditable reason" the occupation of the Four Courts was not brought to an end, Britain would regard the treaty as "having been formally violated," in which case the British would feel free to put their own troops into action.

The Commander-in-Chief of British forces in Ireland, General Nevil Macready, was called to London. But he strongly opposed any British attempt to force Rory O'Connor and the Republican Army out of the Four Courts. Macready warned that a British attack would unite the treaty faction in Ireland with the Republicans and would once again turn the whole Irish people against Britain. The British cabinet finally took the same view, but offered the Provisional Government artillery and other weapons to accomplish the deed, and demanded "that the necessary action will be taken by your government without delay."

In Dublin the Provisional Government called a meeting of all its military and political leaders, presided over by Arthur Griffith. He had been urging the seizure of the Four Courts for a long time, arguing that troubles throughout Ireland would continue as long as a Republican Army, in open defiance of all government, mocked the law itself by making its headquarters in buildings that were the center of the judicial system, but he had been unable to convince Collins.

Now, however, there was the British threat to tear up the treaty they had signed, and the whole Free State Government could be lost. It had won an election, had a constitution, had the strength of British weapons, and Griffith believed the time had come to establish his government's authority and to get on and govern. If excuse were needed, it was found in the kidnaping of the Provisional Government's Deputy Chief-of-Staff, General "Ginger" O'Connell, by the Four Courts Republicans, in reprisal for the capture of one of their chief officers.

The Provisional Government issued an ultimatum for the surrender of the Four Courts. De Valera had urged the garrison there not to provoke an armed clash because there would be little hope of withstanding an artillery attack. But when the ultimatum was delivered to the Four Courts shortly before four o'clock in the morning of June 27, 1922, Rory O'Connor and his men rejected it without reply. With the hopeless gallantry of the Post Office revolutionists of the Easter Rising, they prepared to defend themselves. They would not fire the first shot, but would take up arms if attacked.

Across the River Liffey the Provisional Government had positioned two eighteen-pounder guns, supplied by the British along with the ammunition, and had trained them upon the walls of the Four Courts. Griffith's soldiers filled the streets surrounding the Four Courts buildings. Cars raced up to block off all exits. At seven minutes past four, the Provisional Government attacked and began the Irish Civil War. From across the river, the field guns opened fire.

During all the months of turmoil before, De Valera's one place of personal sanctuary had been his home at Greystones. There, at the seashore removed from the troubles in Dublin, he could relax with Sinead and their six sons and daughters. Their seventh and last child, Terry, was born that shattered year of 1922. With all of De Valera's problems, there had been time for him to be a family man and a father at Greystones, to play ball with his sons, to walk with his children on the beach. The oldest boy, Vivion, although only twelve and still wearing short pants, soon would take to public platforms, speaking in his father's place when De Valera was forced into hiding.

Unaware of what had happened in Dublin, De Valera was spending a quiet evening with his family at Greystones the night civil war began. He was driving into Dublin from there the next morning when his car was stopped on the road by friends who gave him the news. At first he didn't believe the reports could be true. Warned that he might be risking his life to enter the city, he nevertheless went on into Dublin.

"At the bidding of the English," he said in a public statement, "Irishmen are today shooting down on the streets of our capital brother Irishmen. . . . English propaganda will strive to lay the blame for this war on Irishmen, but the world outside must not be deceived. England's threat of war—that and that alone—is responsible. . . . In the face of England's threat of war some of our countrymen yielded. The men who are now being attacked by the forces of the Provisional Government are those who refuse to obey the order to yield—preferring to die. They . . . are not willing that Ireland's independence should be abandoned under the lash of an alien government."

He was the political leader of the Republicans but the Republican Army was now in command and it was as a soldier that De Valera reported to his old Third Battalion of the Dublin Brigade, and was attached to its headquarters in a block of hotels that had been occupied on O'Connell Street. The Republican hope was that the Army could hold Dublin until peace could be restored and De Valera could summon a parliament to declare again for the Republic.

The shelling of the Four Courts went on for two days and nights and into a third day. The buildings caught fire and threatened a store of ammunition, which the men were trying to carry through a tunnel when a great explosion ripped the

Four Courts apart, killing six and wounding two. Some of the defenders were forced into the cellars. Finally an order came from senior officers that "if the Republic is to be saved your surrender is a necessity," so that better defensive positions could be held. The men threw their guns into the flames and marched out of the Four Courts under a flag of truce. One hundred of them, including Rory O'Connor, were taken off to jail as prisoners of the Provisional Government.

When the attack began the objective of the Provisional Government had been to drive O'Connor and his men out of the Four Courts and then to quickly mop up resistance and restore order. They expected the fighting to end with that, but the fighting did not end. Full force was turned upon the hotels where De Valera, Brugha and other Republican leaders were, and where the Republican Army had made emergency head-quarters.

As one building after another was shattered, De Valera and the rest finally were driven into the Hamman Hotel. Under the bombardment, they could not hold out much longer. A decision was made that Brugha and a small garrison would try to hold the remaining building while De Valera, Austin Stack and others escaped to organize resistance throughout Ireland.

With the understanding that Brugha would surrender as soon as those who would carry on the defense of the Republic were safe, De Valera and the rest got out of the building. He made his way unrecognized, through the streets and across a bridge to the other side of the river, and was concealed in a house where he had been expected. Word was sent to Brugha to give up the hotel, without loss of life if possible.

Brugha, with seventeen men, had held out under two days of attack, until the buildings around him had been shelled to rubble and part of the hotel itself was burning. He fought on through most of a third day, until the walls threatened to collapse, but finally called his men together and ordered them to surrender. Expecting him to join them, they gave themselves up and were herded into a lane behind the hotel.

Suddenly Brugha appeared in the doorway, a small smoke-blackened figure, with a revolver in each hand, raised against the pointing rifles of the attacking troops. "Surrender!" he was ordered. "Never!" he shouted back. Firing his two revolvers, he stepped into the volley of shots and fell fatally wounded. It was Brugha's last desperate gesture to arouse Ireland to fight as he had for the Republic, and to die rather than give it up.

Dublin's fighting ended after eight days. Three hundred men had been wounded and sixty killed. A block of O'Connell Street lay in ruins, just as the opposite side of it had been shattered by British guns in the Revolution of 1916. Republicans, in the spirit of revolution, but against other Irishmen now instead of British, were about to wage another guerilla war in the country-side to which De Valera had escaped.

CHAPTER 14

De Valera once again was a man on the run, moving secretly from place to place, in danger of being captured or shot. He was the leader of the Republican cause, but not of its Army, whose commanders sometimes refused to listen to him. He made his way to Clonmel in the south of Ireland, where he served as an adjutant while Chief-of-Staff Liam Lynch moved on out to establish a headquarters at Fermoy.

Republican forces were strongly entrenched in the area at the start of the Civil War, holding the counties of Waterford, Tipperary, Cork, Kerry and most of Wexford. But the Provisional Government sent heavily equipped troops around Ireland to make landings from the sea, and the outflanked and poorly supplied Republicans were forced to evacuate one town after another, burning their barracks, blowing up bridges, attempting to block roads as they retreated. When Fermoy fell in August, 1922, the Republican troops, and De Valera with them, took to the surrounding hills, and there was none of Ireland that remained in Republican control.

De Valera figured the chance for victory was too slight to continue the war at the price Ireland would have to pay in suffering. He recommended seeking terms of peace and a truce under which fighting would cease. But the Army commanders, convinced they could still win a guerilla war, rejected his advice. The fighting went on for eight more months, with the whole nature of it changed.

Open warfare was at an end. There were no longer battles and land battlefronts. The war became a matching of acts of violence, lawlessness, brutality on both sides, a war nobody could win because Ireland itself was the ultimate victim. The Republican Army split up into bands of roving men who mostly made their own decisions, striking where they could against the Provisional Government that held the counties and the towns. As the British had before, the Provisional Government branded the Republicans "criminal outlaws," shot suspects on sight, threw captured men into jail without trial, hurriedly and secretly executed some. It was a war of family against family, in which the soldiers hardly knew which was foe or friend.

The Provisional Government simply ignored the authority of the old Dail and left it standing, never dissolved, as they went on to form their own new assembly as "The House of Parliament to which the Provisional Government is to be responsible." Arthur Griffith and fifteen others, only seven of whom had been members of his administration under the Dail, issued the notice that summoned the new parliament. Among the signers were future President Cosgrave and the future strong man of his Free State Government, Kevin O'Higgins.

Griffith had reached the height of his power and success at the age of fifty. From Revolution to Civil War, he had fought for what he considered best for Ireland without ever firing a single shot himself. But overwork and worry over the war had put such a strain on him that on August 12 he suffered a heart attack and died within a few hours.

Ten days later, Michael Collins, who had become commander of the Provisional Government's military forces, was in a car that was part of an armed convoy traveling over a country road in his native County Cork. Five Republican soldiers who had been waiting in ambush saw the cars and opened fire. Collins might have escaped, but decided to make a fight of it. He and his officers threw themselves to the ground and returned the fire. Collins was shot through the head and killed.

Not long before, Harry Boland, who had been Collins' close friend as well as De Valera's, was fatally shot by Provisional Government soldiers who broke into his hotel room. Ironically, Boland had been the man who helped bring Collins and De Valera together for the election pact discussions, in the unsuccessful attempt to prevent the Civil War.

Erskine Childers, the gun-running hero of Easter Week and long the Republic's chief publicist, soon was captured by Provisional troops and executed by a firing squad. Rory O'Connor and the three other top Republican officers of the Four Courts garrison, in jail since their surrender, were shot to death without trial in what was announced as "a reprisal . . . a solemn warning" to Republicans who had been threatening the lives of Provisional Government deputies. Seventy-seven prisoners in various parts of Ireland were executed by the Free Staters during the months of war in an attempt to terrorize Republicans into halting their own acts of terror.

De Valera tried again in September to find some political settlement. He asked Republican Army commander Liam Lynch and other Army officers to meet with him so Republican military and civil leaders could decide their policy together. But Lynch, wanting no civilian control of the Army, put off the meeting and all but ignored De Valera's messages.

At the risk of being captured, De Valera made his way from the South up to Dublin. There, after secret arrangements on both sides, he and the Provisional Government's Defense Minister, Richard Mulcahy, had a private talk, but could reach no agreement. Mulcahy insisted no Republicans could be seated in the new parliament unless they took the oath; De Valera said that was impossible.

Holding that the legitimate government was still the undissolved Dail, De Valera advised Republican members not to attend the "illegally summoned" new parliament. With Republican members absent, the Provisional Government's assembly met, accepted best wishes from the King's representative in Ireland, and elected William Cosgrave its new President.

Republican deputies held their own secret parliament in Dublin in October and elected De Valera "President of the Republic and Chief Executive of the State." He formed an emergency government, and the Republican Army finally was brought in under it so that officially, at least, the Council of State and not the Army was in control of Republican policy. But while the Army pledged its allegiance to the Council, it also reserved the right to remain "the final custodians of the Republic" in deciding what peace terms it might accept. Since De Valera's Council had little chance of actually functioning as a government, although its members considered it the only "legitimate" government, his election as President served as a protest more than anything else.

The Provisional Government was established and Britain was about to give its formal recognition to the Free State. Its military forces had an inexhaustible supply of war materials from England available, while the disorganized Republican Army was running out of men and munitions. Surrender was only a matter of time, but the Republican Army command would not admit it, and the war dragged on into 1923, with cruelties and brutalities increasing with the determination of the Free Staters to hurry the inevitable, and with the desperation of Republicans to defend their cause to the last of their fading strength.

De Valera tried to operate his government from a downtown Dublin building, where a Republican staff worked, hampered by frequent raids and searches. In January, 1923, he issued a statement deploring the disastrous continuance of the war, "the ever-rising tide of bitterness . . . a bitterness that might persist for generations—the mutual nullification of effort, the vanishing of the common dreams of national regeneration and reconstruction . . . the final despair as each tried ruthlessly and recklessly by the policy of blood and iron to extricate themselves from an impossible position."

"All this," he said, "should have been clearly before the eyes of those who have taken upon themselves the leadership of the nation." They should have realized that "young men who were fighting and daily risking their lives to uphold the Republic . . . would resist to the death . . . the dictated partition of our country, its forced inclusion in the British Empire, the surrender of our sovereignty, the repudiation of our declared independence, and the acceptance of England's King" that "made Civil War inevitable."

By early spring of 1923 the struggle was burning itself out. De Valera went in March to a remote mountain cottage in Waterford County's Nier Valley to meet for four days with the Republican Army command and suggested definite terms of peace. The Army officers were divided, and the Army rejected immediate surrender but authorized him to prepare peace proposals for further discussion.

On April 10, during a skirmish in Tipperary's mountains, Liam Lynch was wounded and taken prisoner. The Republican Army chief died during the night. His death finally broke the heart of Republican resistance. Ireland's Civil War came to an end on May 24, 1923, when the Republican command ordered its Army to cease fire and "dump arms."

It was an indefinite end, with no surrender, no terms. De Valera had proposed terms; Cosgrave had rejected them.

There was no signed armistice, no agreement. Civil War had settled nothing politically between the Free State and the Republic.

One force had exhausted the other and the Free State had come to the end of the war in power, with British endorsement and with a margin of popular support. The defeated soldiers "dumped" their weapons by hiding them away, not surrendering them, and then simply quit and went home. The Free State, with twelve thousand Republicans already in prisons, began rounding up others and jailing them as an "Act of Public Safety" necessary to restore order.

"The Republic can no longer be defended successfully by your arms," De Valera said in a proclamation to the soldiers. "Further sacrifice of life would now be vain. Military victory must be allowed to rest for the moment with those who have destroyed the Republic. Other means must be sought to safeguard the nation's right. Do not let sorrow overwhelm you. Your efforts and the sacrifices of your dead comrades in this forlorn hope will surely bear fruit . . .

"Seven years of intense effort have exhausted our people," he said. "If they have turned aside and have not given you the active support which alone could bring you victory . . . it is because they are weary and need a rest. A little time and you will see them recover and rally again to the standard. . . . When they are ready, you will be."

Hundreds on both sides had been killed, several thousand wounded, thousands were unemployed, hundreds of thousands of farm acres were out of cultivation, millions of pounds of property had been damaged. But the psychological wounds were far deeper. The bitterness of Civil War was to last half a century, dividing Ireland's political life. Just as in the United States, where some Americans went on fighting the issues of its Civil War with words long after war ended, so in Ireland men would passionately blame De Valera or Cosgrave, Griffith or Collins, and all on either side with them. Partition, too, divided the country, not only at its land border, but in the never-healed festering of the great wound it left, with its severed part yet bleeding.

Ireland's Civil War was in the sad pattern that the 20th Century was to spread over the world in Asia, Latin America and Africa, as other peoples after Ireland freed themselves from imperialism or colonial bonds, groped toward stability and drifted into war against their own. But in Ireland it was a war with its issues unresolved. For centuries the British had taught the Irish the rule of force and contempt for any authority without it, and force ruled yet for a time.

The Irish Free State, seeking a clearer mandate from the people, called for a general election in August, 1923. With most of the Republican leaders in jail, and with De Valera and others subject to arrest, it was hardly the "free election" that had been promised. Republican election offices operating under the old Sinn Fein banner were raided, literature was seized, voter registration lists were withheld, speakers were intimidated. Under "such conditions of suppression," De Valera expected only a minority of Republicans to be elected. He announced that those who were elected would consider themselves denied their seats in the Free State Parliament.

"They will refuse to take any oath of allegiance to the King of England, will meet apart, and act together as a separate body," he said, "working along Sinn Fein lines for the honor and welfare of our country." The war, he declared, "so far as we are concerned, is finished," but "politically we shall continue to deny the right . . . of any foreign authority in Ireland" and "in particular we shall refuse to admit that our country may be carved up and partitioned."

He ran for election in what had always been his political

stronghold of County Clare. His opponent was his old commander of the Volunteers and English prison-mate, Eoin MacNeill, who had become a leading member of Cosgrave's Free State Government. Despite warnings that De Valera would be silenced if he dared to campaign in public, he promised to speak in the town of Ennis on August 15. "I will be with them," he said, "and nothing but a bullet will stop me."

Newspaper correspondents as well as Free State troops and intelligence agents crowded into the market place at Ennis. De Valera suddenly appeared, riding down the street in an open touring car, while a band played *The Soldier's Song*. He reached the platform and began to speak. "I have always preached," he started to say, "that if we stand together and are united, we can achieve complete independence—"

Free State soldiers with fixed bayonets moved in, followed by an armored car, and shots were fired over the crowd. They were blank shots, according to a later official report, but a girl was wounded by one. As people stampeded for safety, De Valera, shouting at the soldiers to stop firing, was thrown down on the platform. Uninjured, he struggled to his feet, and as the soldiers raised their guns to fire upon the people again, he halted them by going down to them.

Arrested, he was taken to Dublin's Arbour Hill Barracks. Without being charged or tried, he was kept a prisoner of the Free State for nearly a year. Twelve days after his arrest, the Irish people voted, and the majority vote went to Cosgrave's Free State party. De Valera's party actually picked up eight more seats than it had before the Civil War, for a total of 44, and in County Clare De Valera defeated MacNeill, but the Free State took a national total of 63 seats out of 153.

Returned to power, Cosgrave was reelected President by the Free State Dail, and Kevin O'Higgins, soon to become both the most admired and the most hated man in Cosgrave's administration, was made Vice-President. From prison, De Valera commented caustically, "Those who talk about democracy cannot say, I think, that democracy . . . got very much of a chance."

Cosgrave had a clear majority in the Dail only because the elected Sinn Fein deputies of De Valera's party, refusing to take the oath to the King, were not seated in it. But the fact remained that the Free State Government now had been firmly established with substantial popular support and with British recognition. Preserving the forms under which democracy could develop, it walked a careful line to prevent the emergence of either a police state or a military dictatorship. It put down an army mutiny, took harsh measures to crush Republican resistance, and went about the tasks of trying to restore normal living conditions to a war-shattered country.

Gradually it began releasing its political prisoners, but De Valera was among the last to be let out. He finally was set free on July 16, 1924, at a time when controversy over the boundaries of partitioned Ulster had reached a national crisis. Many Irishmen still hoped that the Boundary Commission set up under the treaty with England would give enough of Ulster to the South so that the shrunken North would be forced to decide it had to unite with the rest of Ireland. But Ulster threatened war against the South rather than give up "a single inch" of its six counties.

While the furious debate raged, there were elections in Northern Ireland in October, 1924, and De Valera decided to go North to campaign for candidates there who were against partition. He was warned that he would be arrested if he set foot across the border. Defying the warning, he went to speak at a meeting at Newry in Ulster's County Down. The Ulstermen seized him, held him overnight, and dumped him back on the Free State side of the border. Almost as soon as they dropped him there, De Valera secretly made his way back across the border to speak in the city of Derry. Arrested a second time, he was taken to Belfast, put on trial, and sentenced to a month in Belfast jail.

By the time he was back in Dublin, the Free State was making an agreement with the British to end the threat of war with Ulster and also to settle the question of debt payments to England so as to provide what Cosgrave called the "basis of a sure and lasting peace." Although Boundary Commission arguments were to go on for a long time, through many complications, the Free State agreement amounted to letting the North keep its six counties. Britain's debt claims were to be met with long-term payments.

Cosgrave's party carried the partition and debt bill through the Dail by a slim vote. Because there was no real opposition, it also put other measures through, such as a law to deny government jobs to Republicans who refused to take the oath to the King._If the Republican members had been in the Dail, they could have blocked such laws, but it became obvious to De Valera that as long as they held themselves outside the Dail, the Free State could enact almost any legislation it wished.

The Republicans, still claiming to be the only legitimate government, actually had been reduced to a public protest group that could only pass resolutions, while Cosgrave's government made the laws. During his months in jail, De Valera had done some hard thinking about the country's political future and his own. Always in him there had been two driving forces, the rebel side by side with the man who had said, "There is a definite constitutional way . . ."

He could not ignore the realities. The Free State was in power and the public was in no mood to support any forced restoration of the Republic. As long as his party stayed out of the Dail, instead of working for Republican goals within the Dail as an active opposition party, it would have no real voice in Ireland's decisions. But in his party there were extreme Republican factions.

De Valera began to suggest ways to remove the oath to the King, so Sinn Fein deputies could take their place in the national assembly as elected representatives of the people. The extreme Republicans who still wanted to fight, turned against him and he lost the leadership support of Sinn Fein. The diehards of the Irish Republican Army withdrew their allegiance to him.

Cosgrave's government had consolidated the treaty position. Partition appeared fixed. The British Governor General, as the King's representative, occupied Dublin's Vice-Regal Lodge, with the veto power of the Crown. English debts were fixed upon Ireland. Irish ports were in the hands of the British Navy. Free State Ministers, attired in Court dress, attended the social functions of Buckingham Palace. British Imperialism had reestablished itself in Ireland's social life.

It seemed to many that De Valera was a defeated and discredited political leader, destined to pursue the dream of an independent Irish Republic to a fading end. Few saw more than a forlorn wish in his prediction that, given time, the Irish people would rally again to the Republican cause. Fewer thought there was any chance that he would lead them.

He had become low man on the political ladder, still popular personally, but that he would ever climb to the top again seemed doubtful. Plainly, he was a man who had lost, just as the Republic had lost. But De Valera, the revolutionary, was about to start his second life, as De Valera the statesman, who also would give another life to the Republic.

CHAPTER 15

"Today we are making a new start for another attempt to get the nation out of the paralyzing treaty dilemma," De Valera told a gathering at Dublin's La Scala Theatre on May 16, 1926. As a man who had not lost faith in the ideal of a Republic, he did not intend to stand by and watch the movement "degenerate . . . to an empty formalism." The "duty of Republicans is to my mind clear," he said. "They must . . . secure common action by getting into position along the most likely line of the nation's advance."

He had left Sinn Fein to found a new political party, Fianna Fail (Warriors of Ireland), and intended to lead elected Republican deputies into the Free State Dail. Whether it was "legitimate" or not, the Dail was "in control of the actual powers of government," and as long as Republicans held themselves outside of it "one-half the electorate was shut out from having an effective voice." His plan was to find constitutional means of destroying the oath of allegiance to the King so that Republicans could take their seats in the Dail.

For years, he had been a leader of revolution; now he meant

to lead the revolutionists into the established government, to make use of the Free State Dail itself so as to achieve "the full political independence we aspire to" by democratic means. Once the oath was destroyed, he foresaw "cutting the bonds of foreign interference one by one," and while waiting for full independence, "the Republican deputies would be able to take an effective part in improving the social and material conditions of the people."

He called on the people to follow the new party out of the political wilderness and into direct political action, to win control of the Free State Dail by election. Fianna Fail pledged itself to assert "the right of the nation to its complete freedom, to oppose all claims of any foreign power to dictate . . . or to interfere in any way in the government of Ireland," to bring partition to an end, to remove "all acts of subservience," and "to replace the Free State Constitution, with all its articles dictated by England, with a Constitution freely framed by the representatives of the people."

Fianna Fail opened its first headquarters in two small rooms, equipped with a couple of tables and a few chairs and a type-writer, in an office building across from the General Post Office, where the Republic had been proclaimed in arms. There, De Valera took charge of the new democratic rising, which was to be accomplished with votes instead of guns. He drove himself to the office each day in a rattling old Ford car. As a way of helping his children get to know the country, he took the older ones along with him on his speaking tours. The family was about to move into a new home in suburban Black-rock.

Within six months the new party gained such a following that five hundred delegates turned out for its first convention in November. But to the establishment, De Valera and the Republicans were still "wild-eyed" revolutionists, branded "socialists" and "communists" by some of the protectors of the status quo because of demands for social legislation and farm and industrial reforms, and because of Fianna Fail's declared intent to do away with the trappings of royalty and to nullify the treaty, step by step. Even moderate social reforms seemed radical to many in those days when few governments in the world had much interest in improving the lives of the people. Fianna Fail's strongest support was from rural districts and the labouring class.

Dublin's newspapers were so solidly against De Valera that Fianna Fail found it impossible to present its views, and had to depend on pamphlets and handbills. All through the years of Revolution and Civil War, when the newspapers were just as strongly anti-Republican and pro-British, De Valera had dreamed of having a newspaper that would "tell the truth." Now, when success depended entirely upon arousing "the enthusiasm and energy that springs from the passionate feeling of the people," the dream became a political necessity. He turned, as Republicans always had, for help from Ireland's friends in America.

De Valera went to the United States early in 1927 to raise the funds for a newspaper, which he would control himself as managing director. Hundreds of Irish-Americans invested small amounts to become shareholders. During the trip, he was able to spend some time in Rochester with his recently widowed mother. He returned to Ireland in May with enough money to launch the new daily paper, although it wasn't until late 1931 that the first edition of what was to become the highly success-ful *Irish Press* was published. Mrs. Margaret Pearse, the mother of Patrick Pearse, the revered patriot leader of the Easter Rising, pushed the button to start the presses rolling. Dublin, for the first time, had a big-circulation newspaper to present the views of Fianna Fail, and to stress Irish culture and customs as well as independence.

De Valera came back to Ireland in time to lead the campaign

for Fianna Fail's first test at the polls in the general election of June, 1927. Pledged to enter the Dail if they did not have to take the oath of allegiance to the King, the Republicans came within two seats of winning. Cosgrave's Free State party, Cumann na nGaedheal (Clan of the Gaels), won 46 seats, but De Valera's Fianna Fail won an impressive 44. The capture of the remaining seats by a number of minor party candidates meant that the Cosgrave administration had lost its clear majority even among those who accepted the oath.

De Valera announced that the Fianna Fail deputies intended to claim the seats to which they had been elected. When the new Dail opened on June 23, 1927, he and his deputies presented themselves at Leinster House and tried to enter. In a dramatic confrontation, they were halted by the Clerk of the Dail, who informed them he had "a little formality" for them to comply with first: taking the required oath. They refused and the doors of the Dail were locked against them.

With the forty-four Fianna Fail deputies excluded, the Dail again elected Cosgrave President of the Executive Council. But there was strong opposition from the Labour Party and others, and the Dail was all but deadlocked by tense emotional debate that challenged the administration. Government was uncertain and forces of violence again threatened the country.

De Valera started a suit to test the oath in the High Court. He and Fianna Fail also began a nationwide campaign to force a referendum on the question, but Cosgrave's administration rushed to put legislation through the Dail to change the Free State Constitution so no plebiscite could be held unless the 'De Valera men first took the oath and were seated in the Dail. Cosgrave's supporters claimed they were merely trying to compel Fianna Fail to accept a responsible role within the parliamentary system.

Sinn Fein, which had been all but wiped out as a political

party by winning only five seats in the election, still held to the old Republican position of keeping itself outside any Free State government. The Irish Republican Army, which had also turned from De Valera when he decided to wage a constitutional fight for a Republic, had become an underground military organization, still dedicated to the use of force. With at least 15,000 men determined to fight on against the Free State, the treaty and partition, the I.R.A. began to take out of hiding the weapons that had been "dumped" at the time of the Civil War's cease-fire. Others turned again to guns. There were shooting incidents, attacks on police barracks, frightening reminders to the nation of how close it still was to the violence of Civil War.

Cosgrave's young Minister of Justice, Kevin O'Higgins, the Vice-President of the Executive Council, had been in charge of keeping public order, and he had used strong-armed methods in dealing with the Free State's own police and army as well as with rebellious Republicans. He also was the most impressive member of the Cosgrave administration, a policy-maker in domestic affairs and its brilliant spokesman in British Empire conferences.

The uncertainty and doubt that hung over Ireland's insecure new government changed to horror and anger on Sunday morning, July 10, 1927. O'Higgins, on his way to church, without his usual bodyguard, was shot to death in front of his Dublin home. His assassins escaped, apparently in a stolen car, and no evidence was ever produced to bring charges against anyone. There were those who blamed disgruntled officers of the Free State army; others who blamed the I.R.A.

De Valera immediately denounced the assassination as plain murder, totally inexcusable for any reason. "I am confident that no Republican organization was responsible for it or would give it any countenance," he said. "It is a crime that cuts at the root of representative government and no one who realizes what the crime means can do otherwise than deplore and condemn it."

Shocked by the assassination, Cosgrave and his ministers saw in it evidence of the lawlessness rising on all sides to threaten orderly Free State government. They acted swiftly to put through a drastic public safety law to give authorities the widest powers of search and arrest in dealing with illegal organizations and individuals. Then they moved to put through another bill, offered to guarantee the future stablilty of government but aimed politically and directly at De Valera and Fianna Fail.

It was an electoral amendment act, under which no candidate could be nominated in any parliamentary election unless he swore in advance that if elected he would take the oath of allegiance to the King. De Valera and his party, already barred from the Dail because of the oath, would now be barred from even running for election. Unless they took the oath, their seats in the Dail would be declared vacant and they would face political extinction.

For the nation, it was a crisis of government; for De Valera and his deputies, it was a crisis of conscience. Taking the oath would mean going back on everything they had said and done since the signing of the treaty, through the years of Civil War, in the campaigning of Fianna Fail itself. But the time for any effective protest outside the Dail had passed. The only way now to keep independence alive was to enter the Dail, dismantle the Constitution of the Free State, and clear the way for a Republic.

De Valera knew that if he gave in he would be condemned by Republican extremists, that his political enemies would make the most of it, that some would call him inconsistent, dishonest or worse. His decision took moral courage, but his vision was on the larger goal. He had faith in the people to understand and to support him, to realize that he was doing not what he wished, but what he had to do to save the Republic.

Perhaps Cosgrave, too, realized that even if it meant risking his own administration by forcing the Republicans into the Dail he would be giving strength and reality to government and to decisions democratically made. De Valera made it clear that he and his deputies were acting under "duress" and because a new civil war would have been "unpardonable." The Free State election law forced them to enter the Dail or to abandon all they meant to achieve. "I grant that what we did was contrary to all our former actions," he said afterwards. "It was a step painful and humiliating for us who had to take it."

They never swore any oath to the King. But they did satisfy the legal formalities, even though they still strongly opposed the oath. On August 10, De Valera and the Republican deputies presented themselves again to the Clerk of the Dail. They also presented him with a declaration that they regarded the requirements of the law as an "empty formality" and that their "only allegiance is to the Irish nation and it will be given to no other power or authority."

The Clerk answered that all he wanted was their names in the registration book. De Valera repeated, "I am not prepared to take the oath. I am not going to take it." He saw a Bible on the table and removed it "so there would be no misunderstanding." But he told the Clerk, "I·am prepared to put my name down here in this book in order to get permission to get into the Dail, and it has no other significance."

He admitted afterwards that there probably was some sort of an oath or promise written across the top of the page, but he deliberately did not read it, and signed only "the way you would sign an autograph." It was enough. He and the Republican deputies were admitted to take their seats as elected members of the Dail.

Five days later, De Valera almost succeeded in putting Cos-

grave's party out of power. His Fianna Fail combined with two
other parties, Labor and the National League, to challenge the
administration, and Labor called for a vote of "no confidence"
in the government. Cosgrave was so certain he was about to be
ousted that on the evening before the vote he gave a farewell
party for his staff. But when the vote was taken it came out a
tie, 71 to 71, and the Speaker of the Dail cast the deciding
vote for the government that saved Cosgrave from defeat. Cosgrave, with his government in a precarious position, dissolved
the Dail and called for a new general election.

In September, 1927, the Irish people went to the polls for the
second time in three months. Both Cosgrave's party and De
Valera's gained in strength and sharply reduced the minor
parties. Fianna Fail won 57 seats and Cosgrave's Cumann
na nGaedheal won 61, which was enough for Cosgrave to
form a new administration with the backing of independents
and the Farmer's Party, a group that represented big land-
owners. De Valera's Fianna Fail would remain the opposition
party in the Dail for the next four years. But with the solid
body of Fianna Fail deputies opposed to him, Cosgrave's clear
predominance was gone.

De Valera led a fighting opposition that constantly kept everything about Free State treaty government under attack, with
the goal of winning the majority support of the people, forming
the next administration, and preparing the way for constitutional creation of the Republic. Fianna Fail promised that the
oath to the King would be removed, along with the British
Governor-General's power as representative of the Crown, and
all the rest of the treaty provisions, including Britain's right to
hold naval bases in Ireland. Sovereignty would be taken from
the King and restored to the people.

To those with low incomes, especially in rural areas that
included half the population, De Valera's attacks against the
economic policies of the Free State promised personal gains as

well as political freedom. Fianna Fail offered a government of the "plain people," less costly, more efficient, less restrictive, with broader social legislation, greater protection for home industry, farm reforms, and increased distribution of large estates to speed return of the land to poor farmers.

The payment of Land Annuities to Britain became a major issue, one that in the immediate years ahead was to change Irish history. It had its beginning in the Irish land wars of the late 19th Century that finally forced the British to adopt a plan under which estates of large landowners were bought and then resold in small parcels to the Irish tenant farmers. The British government advanced the money for the farmers to buy the land, with the loans to be paid back as twice-yearly rents over an annuity period of sixty years.

After the signing of the treaty, when the Free State made its agreement to accept the boundary that partitioned Ulster, Cosgrave announced that in return for the border settlement the British had agreed to write off Ireland's debts. But later agreements left Ireland still owing the Land Annuities and related debts so it was forced to pay millions of pounds a year, a sum estimated at one-fifth of the entire revenues of the Irish state.

De Valera attacked the Cosgrave government's secret agreement with Britain as illegal, one that put an "impossible financial burden" upon Ireland. He wanted the money that was collected as Land Annuities paid, not to the British, but into the Irish treasury. Up in Ulster, the Northern government already was keeping the money, under the Better Government of Ireland Act. The land belonged to the Irish people in the first place, De Valera declared, and there was no reason they should pay the British for farms that were rightfully theirs.

While the conservative Cosgrave government offered the Dail conventional measures, De Valera's opposition presented a sweeping program of economic reform. Against Cosgrave's policy of developing Irish exports, Fianna Fail campaigned for the self-sufficiency of Irish industry and farming. The Free State's drastic measures to restore public order, with the establishment of military tribunals and death penalties to suppress left-wing and Republican extremist groups, added to its unpopularity. People who had suffered enough of such methods under previous British rule were reminded by Fianna Fail that the Free State was still a British government.

Internationally, the Free State already had brought Ireland into the League of Nations, and Cosgrave and its ministers worked at Empire conferences to win the nation greater freedom within the Empire. Irish delegates were among the chief architects of the change in British Commonwealth relations that finally resulted in the Statute of Westminster, approved by Parliament and the King in December, 1931.

Under it, Ireland was declared a Dominion with the "power to repeal or amend any existing or future act of the Parliament of the United Kingdom insofar as the same is part of the law of the Dominion." Winston Churchill fought the change, complaining in the House of Commons that it would give the Irish Dail the right to repudiate the treaty. But Churchill lost, and the way was cleared for De Valera to remove the oath to the King by a simple act of legislation in the Dail, if De Valera and Fianna Fail could win control of the Irish government.

The New York Stock Market crash of 1929 and the worldwide depression that followed it helped tip the political scales in Ireland. As the world depression grew, Ireland's condition became grim. The export markets, upon which the Cosgrave economy was based, dried up and vanished. Exports of bacon, butter, eggs and cattle dropped, factories closed, unemployment spread. For four years, De Valera had been preaching Ireland's need to become self-sufficient, to depend more upon developing its own resources. He offered definite plans for a change. The Free State government seemed to offer only more wage cuts, restrictive measures to cope with depression, less public spending, tightening belts.

Victory for De Valera came in the spring of 1932. His party won 72 seats in the general election and Cosgrave's won only 57. By votes, he had achieved what force could not achieve. By democratic means, the leader of the side that had lost a Civil War had taken power away from the side that had won the War.

When De Valera had predicted at the War's end that, given a little time, the people would rally once again to the Republican cause, few had believed him. But now they had rallied, with their votes, to lift him from the man who ten years before had been the discredited political leader of a defeated revolutionary movement, so that he was at the top of the very government which once had jailed him as a "dangerous criminal."

There were rumors that the Free State army and some of Cosgrave's ministers meant to take to arms themselves rather than turn that government over to De Valera and the revolutionists, and there was fear of a *coup d'etat* to establish a military Free State dictatorship. Forewarned of the plot, De Valera's deputies carried revolvers in their pockets to protect themselves when they took their elected places in the Dail on March 9, 1932.

But William Cosgrave and his top ministers, whatever the Republicans thought of them, were men of democracy. When the time came, Cosgrave made way for the new leader of democratic government, Eamon De Valera. With the support of seven Labor party members, who held the balance of power between the two major parties, De Valera was elected President of the Executive Council of the Dail. He formed an administration in which he put himself in charge of the country's External Affairs.

CHAPTER 16

Two weeks after he took office as President of the Executive Council, De Valera informed the British government that he was abolishing the oath of allegiance to the King. He was carrying out the clear mandate of the Irish people as expressed by their votes, he said in his message to Britain's Secretary of State for the Dominions, James Thomas. The people regarded the oath as "an intolerable burden, a relic of medievalism, a test imposed under the threat of immediate and terrible war," and therefore intended to remove it immediately.

Thomas accused De Valera of threatening the whole treaty settlement. The oath, he said, was mandatory under the treaty and could be changed "only by consent." Constitutional lawyers argued the question and pointed out that the Statute of Westminster cleared the way for removing the oath.

De Valera brushed aside all the legal arguments, one way or the other. He said his decision did not rest upon British law but simply upon the sovereignty of the Irish people. They had the right to alter their Constitution as they saw fit, and they had decided to do so.

He introduced a bill in the Dail not only to remove the oath but to remove restrictions that the treaty imposed upon the Free State Constitution, so it could be opened to democratic amendment by the people. Under the treaty, no law or amendment could be adopted if it conflicted with the terms of the treaty, and De Valera decided that had to go.

His bill to repeal the sections of the Constitution which gave the treaty the force of law, and to demolish the oath which was at the heart of it, was fought in the Dail for months before it finally passed by a margin of eight votes. The British abided by the decision, since there was nothing much else they could do. The oath was abolished and the Constitution opened to amendment. What had been one of the major causes of the Civil War was removed.

De Valera meanwhile made the Irish courts supreme, by removing the right to appeal decisions to the British Privy Council, and he also reduced the position of the King's representative in Ireland, the Governor-General, to almost nothing, pending the time when he could abolish his powers entirely.

The Royal Governor-General, James MacNeill, although personally well-liked, was not only a symbol of the ultimate power of the King and British Parliament, but also an expensive ornament. He held residence in the Vice-Regal Lodge in Phoenix Park, traditional home of the appointed British rulers of Ireland and center of the Crown's social and diplomatic prestige. In theory at least he could veto government decisions in the name of the King.

De Valera cut his position down to acceptable Republican size by a process of erosion and studied insult. When De Valera and his ministers held public receptions, the Governor-General was not among the invited guests. De Valera's ministers ignored invitations to affairs at which the King's representative would be present. When he turned up at diplomatic receptions, they turned their backs on him and walked out. He protested and De Valera asked the British to remove him.

Finally the British agreed, and "on advice of the Executive Council," appointed De Valera's own choice for a new Governor-General. The King's new man was a retired shopkeeper, Daniel Buckley, a Republican veteran of the Easter Rising. He did away with Royal ceremony, performed no duties except for signing routine legal documents, and made his residence in a simple private home in Dublin's suburbs. The great Vice-Regal Lodge was vacated. De Valera not only reduced the power and prestige of the office, but saved the state some £9,000 a year. The greeting of foreign diplomats and visitors was taken over by De Valera himself.

But when De Valera refused to pay the British the millions of pounds a year collected from Irish farmers as Land Annuities, the British fought back. Britain and Ireland were soon locked in a five-year Economic War that cost the Irish millions of pounds in lost exports and seriously hurt Ireland's economy.

When payments became due in July, 1932, De Valera just withheld them. He said Ireland was legally and morally entitled to keep the money. But if the British wanted to question that right he would be willing to submit the matter to international arbitration by the Court of Justice at The Hague.

British Dominions Secretary Thomas hurried to Dublin to talk to De Valera and suggested letting a board made up of members of the Commonwealth decide, but De Valera would accept no board dominated by the British and insisted on having independent arbitration. Britain answered by slapping prohibitively high extra customs duties on Irish products exported to Britain. De Valera struck back by imposing high tariffs on all British goods imported into Ireland.

He told the Irish people that "if the British government should succeed in beating us in this fight, then you could have no freedom, because at every step they could threaten you again, and force you to obey. What is involved is whether the Irish nation is to be free or not."

Although he hadn't planned on an Economic War with Britain, he took advantage of it to launch his own program to make Ireland economically more independent. To reduce the need to import wheat to supply the nation's daily bread and its animal feeds, Irish farmers were encouraged by price supports to raise less cattle and to turn to plowing their land and growing crops. Wheat production was brought from almost nothing to hundreds of thousands of acres. Protected from foreign competition by tariffs and import quotas, hundreds of new factories and workshops were opened and new home industries were supported. Built mostly in rural areas, they provided jobs in the countryside. Under government sponsorship, a national airline and other projects were started, and the peat industry, which one day would fuel most of Ireland's electricity, was developed.

The Economic War, on top of the world depression and continuing troubles at home, hampered the programs and they were not entirely successful. But they did provide a start toward development and they produced business and managerial skills for future years. When war came again to the world, a more self-sufficient Ireland was better able to protect its neutrality. Most important, De Valera provided jobs in a depression, and helped to still the discontent that threatened Ireland's new democracy. He introduced unemployment relief, and a housing program that built some 132,000 new homes.

De Valera dissolved the Dail and called for a general election in January, 1933, to get a new mandate from the people and more legislative backing to put through his programs. He won a clear majority, 77 seats to 48 for Cosgrave's party, but in the wake of his sweeping reelection there was the threat of a fascist uprising as his twice-beaten opponents became desperate to oust him and flirted with a totalitarian Blue Shirt movement.

It was provoked by extremists among De Valera's own Republican followers who took things into their own hands and started breaking up Cosgrave political meetings. Some ex-officers of the Free State army formed a volunteer guard to serve at Cosgrave meetings "to protect the rights of free speech." With membership thrown open to the public, the movement soon claimed 100,000 recruits.

General Eoin O'Duffy, former Free State police commissioner who had been fired by De Valera, became its new leader. He changed its name to the National Guard, adopted blue shirts and military berets as its uniform, and sent his Blue Shirts parading in strength and praising Mussolini, although he himself strongly denied any desire to overthrow the government and set up a military dictatorship.

O'Duffy, a blustery, colorful man with a strong personality appeal, had no political experience and at times seemed unsure what his aims were, except for the desire to oust De Valera and the Republicans and to "end the threat of communism." De Valera called talk of a communist threat in Catholic Ireland "nonsense.' But when O'Duffy summoned his Blue Shirts to gather by special trains for a march past Dublin's government buildings on August 13, 1933, it was not taken lightly. Mussolini's Black Shirt march to power in Rome was too clear an example for De Valera to ignore.

De Valera banned the parade and as a precaution put three hundred police on guard in front of Leinster House and seven hundred more along the route of march. O'Duffy backed down, called off the demonstration, and there was no clash of arms. De Valera then banned the unauthorized wearing of military uniforms in public, the carrying of weapons, and took stern measures to curtail all private armies, including his former comrades of the Irish Republican Army, which he finally had to outlaw.

Meanwhile Cosgrave and his party, whose intentions were more democratic than fascist, decided to hitch themselves to General O'Duffy's popularity in the hope that he could win them enough votes to defeat De Valera at the polls. They combined with a minor party to form a new United Ireland party, soon better known by its Irish name, Fine Gael, of which O'Duffy became president and Cosgrave vice-president. The Blue Shirts were revived, not as a military organization but as a United Ireland youth movement.

For a time, many middle-aged men, including some university professors, adopted the uniform of the Blue Shirt youth movement. Some were moderate in their views; others called for a corporate state and suggested Hitlerite salutes for O'Duffy. But O'Duffy's own somewhat confusing statements became so extreme that Cosgrave followers dropped out, leaders quit, and the movement broke apart. Within about a year, the Blue Shirts faded. Instead of ousting De Valera, they had greatly increased his popularity as a defender of democracy.

Cosgrave's party, regretting its bad political gamble in backing O'Duffy, once more became pretty much the party it had always been before Cumann na nGaedheal traded its name for the new one of Fine Gael, which it kept. Ireland gradually settled back into a democratic parliamentary system and De Valera's strengthening of government by constitutional means helped dull the appeal of force groups from either the right or the left.

Like America's Franklin Roosevelt with his "fireside chats," De Valera made good use of the radio for direct talks to the Irish people. Most of them spoke of him as "Dev," and when they voted it was more for him than his party. Devout, simple in his tastes, a man who neither smoked nor drank, who had a modest income, who lived in an unpretentious home in Black-rock, and who shunned the high silk hat and striped pants of officialdom for an ordinary soft hat and a business suit, he symbolized what the Irish wanted their leader to be.

Just as he was much admired as "an ordinary family man," his wife Sinead, was the most popular woman in Ireland. She seldom appeared in public and devoted herself to home and family, domestic interests shared by the majority of Irish women.

To the farmers and city laborers who were the backbone of his political strength, De Valera was one of them in thought and manner. He took little pleasure in the theater, seldom saw a movie, did enjoy watching sports events or listening to them on the radio, and also liked to read, poetry as well as history, but not fiction. His greatest pleasure, when he had the time, was just in walking in the open country. Even in the city, he liked to walk, and sometimes would dismiss the driver of his car to walk a mile or two alone on his way to work.

He usually managed to get home to dinner, even on his busiest days, and seldom brought work home with him. When he shut the door to the house behind him, it was to be with his wife and family, and he disliked any but the most urgent official interruptions. The people he and Sinead entertained at home were old family friends, not official guests they were obliged to entertain.

When De Valera left the classroom as a teacher he had given up his own studies, but he took a deep interest in the studies of his sons and daughters, and the atmosphere at home on family weekends often was academic. He debated classical mathematics with his oldest son, Vivion, a student of nuclear physics who was to become an outstanding scientist as well as a barrister, a representative in the Dail, and a newspaper director. De Valera's daughter Mairin was to be a professor of marine biology, his son Eamonn a professor of gynecology, Ruairi a professor of archeology. Daughter Emer would marry a professor, and son Terry would be a solicitor and later a Master of the High Court. Each was encouraged to follow his own interests, but De Valera frequently surprised them with his knowledge in their specialized fields.

His health was always robust, but his eyes had been giving him trouble for some time, and he required medical treatment for them in 1936. That was also a year of personal tragedy, when his son Brian, a promising engineering student, was killed in a horseback riding accident in Phoenix Park. And it was a year when De Valera suddenly was faced with a decision that turned Ireland from a Free State into a Republic in all but name.

Edward VIII, on December 11, 1936, abdicated as Britain's King, so that "at long last" he would be free to marry divorced Mrs. Ernest Simpson, "the woman I love." All Dominion governments had to act on the succession. But De Valera was not about to appoint another English King of Ireland. He acted, as he always had, upon the sovereignty of the Irish people, and he threw the King and Crown out of Ireland.

The Dail was not in session, but De Valera summoned it. He introduced two bills. The first was an amendment to remove every reference to the King and his Governor-General from the Free State Constitution so as to end all authority of the Crown over the legislature, the executive, and all functions within Ireland. The second was an External Relations Act. This accepted the King's abdication for the Irish Free State but did not enthrone any successor. It simply declared that Ireland, at the discretion of its own government, might authorize the King of other Commonwealth nations to act for it in appointing diplomats and making treaties.

Under De Valera's pressure, both bills were passed by the Dail within two days. The Irish Free State had ceased to be one of His Majesty's Dominions. It had become an Associated State, republican in form, with King and Crown finally removed.

De Valera had, in effect, wiped out the whole treaty, except for partition and British naval control of Irish seaports. He had put into operation the plan for External Association that he proposed and that Britain rejected at the start of the treaty talks fifteen years before. Internally there was an independent Ireland, with the sovereignty of the people supreme; externally, Ireland was a Commonwealth associate to a very limited extent, for only as long as it might decide to continue that association.

Ingeniously, he had given the Republicans a republic in fact, but he also had preserved a link with the Commonwealth in the interests of national unity. Those who were against complete separation would be somewhat soothed, a possible way would be left open for uniting the North and South, and he guessed that the British, who had gone far toward loosening Commonwealth relationships, might now be ready to accept External Association.

Before he first took office, De Valera had promised the people "to replace the Free State Constitution, with all its articles dictated by England, with a Constitution freely framed by the representatives of the people." Step by step, from the removal of the oath to this ending of the Free State itself, he had torn apart the old Constitution so nothing but shreds of it were left. Even before King Edward VIII abdicated, De Valera had been drafting a new Constitution, working on it most of the year. It was one of the few times he had brought work home in the evenings, to go over every word of it. The result was to be his most enduring single achievement.

He hoped, in his own words, that the new Constitution would "inspire as well as control, elicit loyalty as well as compel it" and that every citizen would see in it "the sure safeguards of his individual rights as a human being, God-given rights which even the civil powers must not invade."

De Valera's Constitution dealt not only with the structure of government, but in detail with the duties and rights of the family as the basic unit of society, with guarantees of full religious freedom, and with broad social policies. It became a model for the later Constitutions of India, Pakistan and Burma, which borrowed some sections from De Valera almost word for word.

The Constitution called for a new "sovereign, independent and democratic state," to be named Eire (Ireland), and claiming as its territory "the whole island of Ireland," the partitioned North as well as the South. But until the day when the North might be reunited with the rest of Ireland, Eire's laws would apply only to what had been the Free State. God and not the King was recognized as the source of authority, and the Constitution declared that "all powers of government . . . derive, under God, from the people, whose right it is to determine the rulers of the State."

Eire was to have a President, elected by the people as Head of State and as guardian of the Constitution and of their rights. As chief executive and Head of Government, there was to be a Prime Minister, the Taoiseach (Chief). For the most part, the President's duties were symbolic, somewhat like those of a king in a limited monarchy, but the President had special powers to refer any bill to the Supreme Court for constitutional decision, or to withhold his signature from bills in cases when they called for direct approval of the people by referendum. There also was to be a new Senate, to review laws passed by the Dail, with limited power to delay but not to reject them.

Endorsed by the Dail, the Constitution was approved by a national plebiscite on July 1, 1937, and in the same election the people voted De Valera into the chief executive's office as

Taoiseach. Dr. Douglas Hyde, founder of the Gaelic League, poet, professor and a Protestant, was chosen the unopposed first President of Eire.

The British government, after much discussion and consultation among the Dominions, finally decided to accept the whole Irish arrangement. A statement issued from 10 Downing Street said Britain was "prepared to treat the new Constitution as not effecting a fundamental alteration in the position of . . . 'Eire' or 'Ireland' as a member of the British Commonwealth of Nations."

De Valera's view was that if the Commonwealth had developed to such a point that they were willing to accept Ireland's repudiation of allegiance, throwing out the King and establishing a republic, as "not effecting a fundamental alteration," he would not press the matter. "If they want to keep on saying we are in the Empire," he said, "we cannot stop them."

Ireland had its independence and External Association and Britain still considered Ireland entitled to Commonwealth preference. With the status accepted in fact, the twenty years of Irish political revolution against England had come to an end. Statesmanlike diplomacy on both sides was opening the way for better relations.

De Valera announced, early in January, 1938, that there would be a meeting in London between representatives of the two governments "to settle outstanding questions." Among them was the Economic War, partition that was not likely to be settled, and the matter of British-held treaty ports in Ireland.

Under the treaty, Britain had the right to harbor naval vessels in the Irish seaports, and in time of war or international emergency to make use of the ports in whatever way might be required for the defense of the British Isles. With the world rushing toward what was to become the Second World War, the treaty ports became crucial to Ireland's hope to save itself from foreign attack in case of war.

The supreme test of the sovereignty of any nation was whether it had the right to decide for itself about peace or war. De Valera had been deeply concerned, since he first became head of Ireland's government, over the threat of invasion of small nations by big powers, and the violation of their neutrality.

Back in 1932, taking his turn as President of the Council of the League of Nations in Geneva, he had discarded a routine speech reviewing the year's work of the League and had startled its members by asking what the League really had done to preserve world peace during its thirteen years of existence. "A testing time has come," he warned the diplomats. If the League hoped to survive it had to do more than just talk peace; it had to act against the violations of the big powers that flaunted its decisions and it must "say unmistakably that the Covenant of the League is a solemn pact, the obligations of which no state, great or small, will find it possible to ignore."

More than that, De Valera said, it was time to look to the real causes of world unrest, the things that lay beneath the veneer of high diplomacy and the "pressure of powerful national interests." As the League members sat in stony silence, he told them "complacent resolutions cannot satisfy the demand for effective action. We are defendants at the bar of public opinion." He went on:

"One hundred million people are faced with starvation in the midst of a world of plenty—a world where human energy and scientific and mechanical development have reached a stage of potential production capable of meeting many times the peoples' needs. . . . It is our duty here to face this desperate situation frankly and honestly, not as the representatives of States or parties or special interests, but as men who realize that the primary duty of statesmen, national and international, is to plan for the well-being and happiness of their fellows—the plain ordinary human beings in every country who feel and think and suffer. . . .

"The time has come for action. The whole basis of production, distribution, finance and credit requires a complete overhauling. . . . If we shirk any item in this task, if we fail to make the radical changes obviously necessary, if we fail to organize our economic life deliberately and purposely to provide the fundamental needs . . . so that everyone may at least be reasonably housed, clothed and fed, we shall be failing in our duty, and failing cruelly and disastrously."

When Japan's invasions of Manchuria were followed by Mussolini's decision to invade Abyssinia, as the years moved closer to another World War and the big powers did little to protect the small, De Valera again warned the League: "Make no mistake, if on any pretext whatever we were to permit the sovereignty of even the weakest state amongst us to be unjustly taken away, the whole foundation of the League would crumble into dust."

The League failed and after Abyssinia came Hitler's march into the Rhineland. Collective security had broken down and De Valera was convinced that for a small state there was only one way left to save itself from the ruin of war that surely would destroy it. That way was neutrality, but the question for Ireland then was whether it could preserve its neutrality in a world at war if British warships took harbour in its ports.

So De Valera went to London in 1938 to deal with Prime Minister Neville Chamberlain, who was about to be accused of trying to appease the menacing totalitarian states. Chamberlain also was in a mood to appease Ireland, to end the bitterness of centuries, and he and De Valera reached agreement to halt the ruinous Economic War. The Irish government agreed to pay ten million pounds to settle all outstanding debt claims between the two countries. Then, on the last day of the successful negotiations, De Valera brought up the question of returning the Irish naval bases. Perhaps to De Valera's own surprise, Chamberlain agreed that while they were settling everything else, they might as well settle that too.

De Valera's old treaty foe Winston Churchill assailed Chamberlain in the House of Commons. "You are," he accused him, "casting away real and important means of security and survival for vain shadows and ease." But Prime Minister Chamberlain, in the desire to make final political peace with Ireland, signed the agreement for Britain to give up the Irish ports.

De Valera had secured a major diplomatic triumph, one that would make effective Irish neutrality in a Second World War possible. He brought home to his people not only an end to the war of tariffs, but also the promise that they could save their new small democracy through the years when the big powers fought the war of the world. Ireland was to prove by the decision of whether to have war or peace that it was an independent sovereign nation.

CHAPTER 17

Ireland was for the first time facing a "particular obligation of freedom," De Valera said early in 1939, "the obligation of trying to preserve it." The Irish people, he told foreign newspaper correspondents, were "determined to keep our nation out of war."

But in a war that involved most of the world, the infant Irish nation's chances of maintaining strict neutrality between Churchill's England and Hitler's Germany seemed slight. The threat of a Nazi invasion of Ireland was, for a time, very real, and so was the threat of a defensive invasion by the British. It took all of De Valera's considerable diplomatic skill to match one against the other and convince each of them that violating Ireland's neutrality would cost more than it was worth.

He had the people almost solidly behind him from the beginning. Like De Valera, most of the Irish favoured democracy over Hitler's Nazi totalitarianism. But at the same time, Britain was the ancient enemy, from whom Ireland had just wrung independence, and the British held the six partitioned counties of the North which Eire still claimed as its national territory.

Churchill, at the head of Britain's government, was Republican Ireland's personal foe, the champion of Empire who had helped impose the treaty.

"You cannot ask a small nation to fight with you for justice," De Valera later said, in a comment that pretty well summed up Irish feeling, "when you are inflicting an injustice on that small nation."

The day after the Second World War began in September, 1939, with German armies crossing the Polish frontier, De Valera asked the Dail to give him and his government emergency powers "for securing the national safety and preservation of the state." From the outset, strict official neutrality was declared and maintained, although unofficially the country tended to be more on the side of the Allies. He held the delicate diplomatic balance, raised a defensive army of some 250,000 men that backed Ireland's determination to resist invasion from any direction, and kept the economy going under severe hardships.

Ireland had always depended upon Britain for much of its goods and raw materials, and still had to obtain them. But Britain was now one of the belligerent powers, controlling the seas and the sources of supply for Ireland, and could and did apply economic pressures. Sugar, tea, fuel, bread and clothing had to be tightly rationed. Coal for household use disappeared and people had to burn dried turf to heat their homes. Gas, electricity and gasoline for automobiles were added to the ration list and there were scarcities of all ordinary goods.

The flow of raw materials to Ireland's developing new industries was almost entirely cut off so that many factories closed and threw people out of work. Wages were held down by emergency order to prevent inflation, but standards of living fell even for those lucky enough to keep their jobs. De Valera pushed the growing of wheat to new high levels, battled the problem of not having enough fertilizers to maintain the productivity of the soil, and dealt with the desperate need for increased farm labour.

The outlawed Irish Republican Army, reduced to a small but dangerously radical group, was flirting with German spies in its underground war against both the Irish government and Britain, and De Valera worked swiftly to bring it under control by a series of arrests. Strict censorship was imposed on the press to keep newspapers from showing favoritism toward either the British or the Germans. De Valera kept Irish feelings calmed when a German plane bombed Dublin by mistake.

From the start of the war, he tried to maintain strictly impartial dealings with both the British and German ambassadors. He never told anyone, even his cabinet, all that was in his mind, and managed to conceal his own intentions and wishes so that both sides were satisfied with his apparent neutrality. Dramatic incidents brought one ambassador or the other rushing to interview him day and night.

He ended a serious spy scare by putting under arrest an important German agent who arrived in Ireland to establish contacts with the I.R.A. When Hitler wanted to send two Nazi military attaches to work in Dublin's German legation, De Valera prevented it. The German legation also had been operating a radio transmitter to broadcast weather reports from Dublin, but De Valera asked the Germans to make no further use of it and they finally agreed. The transmitter was handed over and quietly put away in a Dublin bank vault for the war's duration.

Ireland's most anxious year was 1940 when Hitler's armies overran the Low Countries and finally France. Germans were in the Channel Islands and were preparing to attack the British mainland. Rumor had it that Nazi divisions were about to land on the Irish coast. "There is but one line of safety for us," De Valera said, "and that is to be ready to resist to the utmost whosoever may attack us."

Army mobilization was increased and Irish troops were paraded through Dublin's streets in a show of force to discourage any invader. On the British side, Churchill complained in the House of Commons that the British Navy was being seriously hampered by not being able to use Irish ports against German submarines operating in the Atlantic. Churchill asked De Valera to permit the use of Irish ports and to allow British troops to enter Ireland to forestall possible German invasion. De Valera refused and answered that any British attempt to violate Ireland's neutrality would be resisted with force, just as any German attempt would be. He made both sides believe him.

When the United States entered the war in December, 1941, thousands of American troops entered Northern Ireland to make it a training base for the coming Allied invasion of Normandy. The rest of Ireland feared for a time that its neutrality might be invaded not by Britain or Germany but by America. De Valera protested the American occupation of Irish territory, but the situation gradually cooled.

Churchill sent De Valera a typically personal note, urging the Irish to enter the war on the British side as a means of uniting the North and South of Ireland. Churchill still had not given up hope of a reunion of Ireland within the Empire and he wrote De Valera that "it is now or never for Orange and Green to unite." But De Valera, not about to listen to any British proposals for discarding Irish independence and neutrality to return to some version of Home Rule, rejected Churchill's discussion that they meet to discuss it. Churchill then encouraged President Roosevelt to help him pressure Ireland into the war and Roosevelt, who had little sympathy for De Valera's neutrality policy, brought heavy pressure.

But the successful Allied invasion of France finally put an end to the war, with Ireland still among the world's only half dozen neutral nations. There was one last bitterness. Churchill, in his Victory Broadcast on May 13, 1945, included a personal attack against his old enemy De Valera. "Owing to the action of Mr. De Valera," Churchill told the world, "the approaches which the Southern Irish ports and airfields could so easily have guarded were closed. . . . This was indeed a deadly moment in our life and if it had not been for the loyalty and friendship of Northern Ireland, we should have been forced to come to close quarters with Mr. De Valera . . ."

De Valera answered in a broadcast from Dublin four days later. "I know the answer I am expected to make," he said, "the answer that first springs to the lips of every man of Irish blood who heard that speech . . . the reply I would have given a quarter of a century ago." But he would not make that kind of a reply. "Allowances can be made for Mr. Churchill's statement, in the first flush of his victory," he said. "No excuse could be found for me in this quieter atmosphere."

He could understand that Churchill "should be irritated when our neutrality stood in the way of what he thought he vitally needed," De Valera went on, but for Churchill to say that "in certain circumstances he would have violated our neutrality and that he would justify his action by Britain's necessity . . . would mean that Britain's necessity would become a moral code and when this necessity became sufficiently great, other people's rights were not to count."

To justify acts of aggression on that score, De Valera said, would mean "no small nation adjoining a great power could ever hope to be permitted to go its own way in peace." He also reminded Churchill that against Britain itself Ireland had been "a small nation that stood alone, not for one year or two, but for several hundred years against aggression . . . a small nation that could never be got to accept defeat."

Ireland, although physically undamaged by war, was in a poor condition when it ended. Discontent fed on continuing shortages of goods, machinery and raw materials. Production and wages lagged while prices and taxes soared. De Valera planned for industrial expansion, poured farm subsidies into increased wheat production, launched programs for home building and rural electrification. But, as in all of Europe, recovery in Ireland was slow. Poor harvests forced the rationing of bread again in 1947 and low fuel supplies temporarily crippled industry and transportation. More than that, the Irish people were restless for a change.

De Valera's personality had dominated Ireland's political life for nearly three decades. From his mind had come almost every important development of the nation. By 1947 his Fianna Fail party had been in control of government for fifteen unbroken years, and his opponents were beginning to wonder if he would remain in power forever. The mood of discontent and the climate for change brought the defeat of two Fianna Fail candidates by a new political party in fall by-elections in 1947.

The new party, Clann na Poblachta (Republican Family), was led by a Republican idealist of the old school of extreme radicals, Sean MacBride, son of one of the men executed after the 1916 Rising. The hard core of his followers included members of the underground Irish Republican Army, and also some young socialists. They attacked De Valera for "betraying" the early revolutionary ideals of the Republican movement, for being too moderate and parliamentary, and promised a swift end to partition and sweeping social reforms to solve most of Ireland's problems.

In a general election early in 1948 the Clann gained ten seats in the Dail, enough to give it a balance of power. De Valera's Fianna Fail remained by far the largest party, but to continue in office it needed minor party support. Leaders of the other parties decided to sink their differences and form a coalition to take the government from him. With no common policy except to oust De Valera, extreme radicals linked forces with extreme conservatives, and brought almost every other political element into the coalition. It included the new Clann, members of Cosgrave's Fine Gael, Labour, Farmers and Independents.

De Valera went out of office and the unlikely coalition managed to hold a shaky majority to keep him out for three years, during which it did achieve some minor reforms before it expired in hectic controversy. The fact that it held together as long as it did was due to the tact of the man named Prime Minister in De Valera's place, a distinguished Dublin lawyer, John Costello.

Instead of relaxing in his temporary retirement, De Valera made a 40,000 mile plane trip around the world in the hope of arousing public support to end the partition of Ireland. He had reached the age of sixty-six and was becoming partially blind, despite a wartime operation that had restored his sight for a time and another soon to be performed that would leave him unable to read but still able to distinguish the shape of objects around him. He concealed his increasingly poor eyesight so well that few people were conscious of it, and it had little effect on the active life he continued to lead.

Seated in the plane's cockpit during his flight to New York early in 1948, he joked with the pilot about how much more comfortable it was to cross the Atlantic that way than when he was a stowaway hidden in the hold of a freighter during the Revolution. He also recalled that the first time he had been up in a plane was with Charles Lindbergh as its pilot. Friends had been trying to get him to fly, but he had joked that he would wait until "Lindy" took him up. Then in 1936 Lindbergh unexpectedly came to Dublin, and as De Valera explained, "My friends kept me to my word."

A large crowd waited to greet him when the plane landed at dawn at La Guardia Airport, and New York gave him a City Hall welcome and a ticker tape parade through its streets. In

Washington he visited President Truman at the White House. Philadelphia, Boston, Chicago and cities across the country to the West Coast welcomed him with parades, receptions and civic honors. On the way, he made several hundred speeches and broadcasts in his "World Appeal Against Partition." From the United States, he flew on to Australia for more speeches, then to Burma, and to India to visit his old friend Premier Nehru and Mrs. Indira Gandhi, and to exchange greetings with other leaders of India's fight for freedom, who spoke of the inspiration of De Valera's own battle for Ireland's independence.

De Valera returned to Dublin to find his opponents about to make a dramatic change in Ireland's relations with the British Commonwealth. Under pressure from its radicals, the conservatives in the new coalition government had decided to declare a Republic of Ireland. In an amazing about-face, men who had spent their whole political life defending the treaty position to keep Ireland within the Commonwealth were now ready to accept the fact that it had been a republic in all but name for the past twelve years, and they intended to give it that name.

Prime Minister Costello hoped to satisfy the extreme Republicans, to "take the gun out of politics" by ending the old treaty arguments, and to make Ireland's republican status clear to the world. De Valera and his party found themselves being politically robbed of credit for the republic he had created. But more as a statesman than a politician, he feared the serious effect the move might have in tightening partition of the North and South.

What De Valera had fought for from the beginning was a Republic of Ireland that would include "the whole island of Ireland." His plan of external association had removed all ties to Empire except for the link that permitted Eire to continue, for as long as it wanted to, to appoint its diplomats and make treaties through the Commonwealth. Now the Costello coalition was asking the Dail to wipe out the External Relations Act of 1936, to declare a Republic of Ireland, and to let its President appoint diplomats.

De Valera had been working toward that goal gradually, but as he explained in debate in the Dail, he had "hesitated about declarations of this sort" and had "left a bridge for a long time" to keep the way open to end partition. "You are not declaring a republic," he told the Dail, "but you are declaring that the state that exists is a republic." He pointed out that "there has been no King of Ireland, either internally or externally since 1936, and certainly not since 1937. . . . The bill does not purport to be establishing a new state."

Because of the partition problem, he questioned the wisdom of such a change. It would be "burning our boats." Yet as the creator of the Republic, he and his party could hardly oppose calling it that. So De Valera and Fianna Fail joined the rest of the Dail in voting to declare the Republic of Ireland, which was proclaimed on April 18, 1949.

As he had feared, the decision was greeted in London by a new act of Parliament, put through under pressure of Ulster's Unionists, which declared that the Republic of Ireland included only the twenty-six counties of the South, and which gave explicit new guarantees to the North. The South finally had put itself outside the Commonwealth, Britain agreed, but "it is hereby declared that Northern Ireland remains a part of His Majesty's Dominions and of the United Kingdom and it is hereby affirmed that in no event will Northern Ireland or any part thereof cease to be a part of . . . the United Kingdom without the consent of the parliament of Northern Ireland."

By 1951 De Valera was back in office as Prime Minister, after the coalition had collapsed in rifts and disputes among its conflicting parties. The election, however, gave him no clear majority, and Fianna Fail held power only with the support of Independents in the Dail. Ireland's political seesaw put De Valera out again in 1954, when Fine Gael and Labour increased their votes. A second coalition government, headed once more by Costello, lasted until 1957.

De Valera waged what was to be his last direct political campaign that year. He had lost none of his campaigning fire at the age of seventy-five. Personally he and Sinead also had a new family of two young children. When his son Vivion's wife died in 1951, De Valera and his wife adopted Vivion's year-old son Eammon and five-year-old daughter Ann, and raised their grandchildren as they had their own sons and daughters. Out on campaign trips or not, De Valera made it a point to schedule speaking engagements so weekends could be spent at home with them. Vivion meanwhile became the new director of the flourishing group of *Irish Press* newspapers.

De Valera carried his party to the greatest election victory it ever had in March, 1957, and with seventy-eight representatives in the Dail to give him a commanding majority he began to put into effect the programs that kept Ireland's voters satisfied enough to leave Fianna Fail in control of the government well into the 1970's.

His election marked the twenty-fifth anniversary of his first taking over of leadership of the Free State and changing it to a Republic. Through all the years and all the troubles, he had led his nation from revolution to stable, constitutional government.

De Valera's two great disappointments were that Ireland remained partitioned, and that despite his every effort the Irish language had not been accepted by the people as the common language of their country. But the time had come for him to retire from active politics, to let others in his party take over government, while he kept a protective hand upon the nation as its President and Head of State.

CHAPTER 18

De Valera did not campaign for the Presidency in 1959. He ran for election against Sean MacEoin, the candidate of the Cosgrave Fine Gael party, but he took no personal part in the campaigning, which he left to the ministers of his government. "The Presidency is above politics," his Deputy Prime Minister Sean Lemass explained, "so it is left to those of us who desire to see him President to urge the people to elect him."

Lemass, about to inherit government leadership, spoke of De Valera's leaving the Dail for the Presidency. "We knew that with the passing of the years it would become necessary for him to leave us," he said. "But despite his loss we can face the future with confidence because his principles are firmly fixed and the work he started will go on."

De Valera had not yet quit politics, however, and on the night before the mid-June election he made his last political speech at a gigantic Fianna Fail rally in Dublin's College Green, not as a Presidential candidate but still as Prime Minister. He had led the party for thirty-three years, since he founded it in 1926, and the thousands of followers who turned out for

171

the parting ovation cheered for ten minutes before they let him speak.

He carefully avoided any mention of his own Presidential candidacy and appealed to the people to back a Constitutional change intended to do away with Ireland's voting system of proportional representation, which had allowed the two weak coalition governments to come into existence. It was an appeal he would lose. The same voters who were to elect him President would decide to keep the voting system they had. But after he finished speaking that night for the amendment, half a dozen party leaders spoke for him from the same platform.

The party's slogan always had been "De Valera and Ireland," but it was changed for the election to "Ireland for De Valera." He had privately told friends months before that whatever the election results were he intended to remove himself from politics, whether as a private citizen or as President. When the official vote count was completed on June 20, 1959, he learned that he had been elected President by a majority of more than 120,000, to succeed Sean O'Kelly, his former deputy who had been President fourteen years.

While congratulations poured in and flashbulbs popped around him, De Valera made a typically dignified statement that it was "an inestimable honor" to be elected "first citizen of this ancient nation." He then resigned as Prime Minister and turned the government over to Lemass, under whose dynamic leadership Ireland's industry and trade were to develop along lines approved by De Valera in the first of a series of sweeping programs for economic expansion. As Head of State, De Valera still would have influence over the affairs of the nation, but he no longer would have any voice in the day-to-day political affairs of government. The forty-six years of his life spent in direct political action were ended.

Before his inauguration, he made a visit to Ennis in County Clare, the district that had first chosen him a candidate for the

Dail years before, while he was still in an English prison, and that had stood by him in every election since. He urged the people of Clare to keep the Irish language and the roots of Irish culture nourished and thanked them for all the years in which they had kept the banner of national freedom and independence "in the front all of the time."

Shortly after noon on Thursday, June 25, he and Sinead entered Dublin Castle, once the seat of the British government that had sentenced him to death as a "dangerous revolutionary," and a fanfare of trumpets announced his arrival for the inauguration ceremony. On the dais surrounded by 350 heads of all branches of government, members of the Dail and Senate, and foreign dignitaries, he took the oath of office in the Castle's St. Patrick's Hall. Trumpets sounded again and outside a twenty-one-gun salute was fired as the tricolor flag of Ireland and his Presidential standard were raised. The *Soldier's Song,* now the national anthem, was sung.

He had been President of the Irish Republic in 1919, when it was a revolutionary government unrecognized anywhere outside of Ireland, and now he was President of the Republic of Ireland, the constitutional government he had helped establish and bring to recognition by the world.

"It is as our head and rightful chief that I now address you," Prime Minister Lemass said to him, "to whom above all other men we owe our freedom to choose for ourselves the President of a sovereign, independent, democratic state. Your name is revered not only at home in Ireland but among the millions . . . in all free nations of the world."

In the Presidential car, escorted by an Army motorcycle guard of honour, De Valera and his wife were driven along a processional route through Dublin to the cheers of those who crowded the sidewalks. At the General Post Office, where the Republic was first proclaimed, they paused to pay tribute to his comrades of the Easter Rising. They were driven then to

Phoenix Park and to what had become The President's House, the former Vice-Regal Lodge of the British Governors-General. There, surrounded by the largest enclosed park in Europe, they would make their home in a centuries-old white mansion, shaded by trees planted by Queen Victoria.

They had a luncheon reception there, and that night another Presidential reception at Dublin Castle, attended by two thousand guests. Among the heads of other governments who sent messages was America's President Eisenhower, who said De Valera's inauguration was "a fitting tribute to your long years of service to your country."

As President, De Valera was guardian of the Constitution of which he had been the author, and was the channel through which its authority flowed. Acting on the advice of the Dail, he would appoint the Prime Minister, department heads and judges, command the Army, summon and dissolve the Dail, sign bills into law, or refuse to sign if he suspected a bill infringed the Constitution.

His power as President was real but not absolute, since it depended on the advice of the Dail, or in some cases on referendum or decision by the Supreme Court. Many of his duties were normally ceremonial, but his Presidency had the vital purpose of guarding against any break in the continuity of government and against any temptation on the part of the parliament to exceed its legitimate powers. He would appoint Ireland's ambassadors and receive the ambassadors to Ireland from foreign nations, and would have particular influence in its international affairs.

Despite the failure of the League of Nations, De Valera had been ready for the "second experiment" in world cooperation when the United Nations began, and while he was Prime Minister back in 1946 his government had applied for membership, only to be blocked by vetoes of the Soviet Union until 1955. As

President, De Valera was to see Ireland's pioneer resolution for an agreement to halt the further spread of nuclear weapons adopted by the United Nations. Ireland would send troops on United Nations' peace-keeping operations and observer missions to the Congo, Cyprus, Lebanon, the Middle East and the Indo-Pakistan border. During De Valera's terms as President, Ireland would consistently condemn the Apartheid policies of the Government of South Africa, approve economic sanctions against Southern Rhodesia, and would work toward giving more attention to economic questions in the newly developing countries. His country would be among the first to take an active interest in the European Economic Community.

As Presidential salaries went, his salary of less than £10,000 a year was modest, and the whole upkeep of the Presidential establishment was only around £14,500 a year. But the vast official President's House in Phoenix Park that he was obliged to live in was somewhat too grand for his taste. As a man who frequently had slept on a cot in a jail cell, and as one who preferred simplicity in all things, he often told friends that if he had his choice he would prefer to live in a little farmhouse somewhere in the country.

"The Ireland we have dreamed of," he once said, "would be the home of a people who valued material wealth only as a basis of right living, a people who were satisfied with frugal comfort and who devoted their leisure to things of the spirit."

He had little liking for the mass-produced and plastic world, or for many of the changes that were coming to a modernized Ireland and a cosmopolitan Dublin. But he kept himself well-informed about what was happening in Ireland and in the world. Although he was removed from the daily battles of politics, few of their subtleties escaped him. He was far from being a Presidential hermit in the big and sometimes lonely mansion.

As the world's most elder senior statesman he maintained an active, taxing schedule of ceremonial as well as official duties. Courtly and charming in manner, he entertained visiting leaders of the world. He made frequent trips, such as to Rome with his wife and two of his grown children for an audience with the Pope, to the United States, and elsewhere. Ramrod straight and eagle-profiled, he was the personification of living legend as he spoke at public ceremonies honoring heroes who had been his comrades and who had now passed into Ireland's history.

His private office was shelved with classics and other books he loved and no longer could read because of near-blindness, but he was an avid radio listener and later enjoyed television, especially watching ball games. "He can't half see it," a close friend said, "but it's amazing how much he gets out of TV." Visitors to his office seldom were aware he could hardly see them. He had a keen memory for names and for precise details of events that had happened years before, and also an ability to carry on an informed conversation on almost any current subject that was brought up.

De Valera's weekends still were family times, with visits by some of his four living sons and two daughters, and later by his eighteen grandchildren and one great-grandchild. His adopted granddaughter Ann spent much of her time at Phoenix Park.

When his first term as President ended, he ran for a second seven-year term in 1966, at the age of eighty-four, against a forty-nine-year-old opponent, T. F. O'Higgins, a relatively little-known lawyer, the candidate of the Fine Gael party. William Cosgrave, the old leader of the opposition to De Valera had died the year before at the age of eighty-five and Fine Gael's leadership had passed to his son, Liam.

De Valera decided once again not to campaign personally. He said it would not be good constitutional practice for him, while holding the office of President, to participate in a campaign into which political issues would be introduced. "The Presidency is not a political party office," he said. "To go out and campaign would be impossible without going into party politics."

But political issues were brought up, by both sides, and O'Higgins called for Presidential leadership with "more modern vision of the problems of the country." De Valera won, mainly because the rural areas gave him a clear majority, but the contest was much closer than expected. Young O'Higgins captured Dublin and Cork, and De Valera was reelected by a margin of only ten thousand votes out of well over a million.

It had been only a half-century since the Easter Rising, less than thirty years since De Valera's Constitution had given the Irish people the right to select their own President. But Ireland had come to take established government so much for granted that one-third of the electorate did not even bother to vote.

There would have to be a complete change in the Constitution, De Valera told reporters afterwards, before a President of Ireland could do many of the things some people suggested he should do. As things stood, no President could directly interfere with government policy. "If his opinions are *asked,* he can give them," he said, "but he has to take the advice of the government and not give it."

He reminded them that years before, when the Constitution was being battled through the Dail, there had been strong opposition to letting the President take any part in the daily operations of government, for fear he might have something like dictatorial powers because he would not be subject to open questioning. That was why the President had been separated from government as the Head of State.

But the government itself soon changed. Sean Lemass, the architect of Ireland's economic recovery and one of the most progressive Irish leaders since independence, but a man of sixty-seven and one of those who had been in the Rising of

1916, stepped down as Prime Minister. His place at the head of government and also as leader of Fianna Fail was taken by younger Jack Lynch, the first Prime Minister of a post-Civil War generation.

De Valera continued as Head of State, actively and efficiently carrying out his second term, still President into the 1970's. Under the Constitution, only two terms were allowed. He did his work well in the big President's House, but said again that if he could choose, he would rather live in the country. "I was brought up in the country," he said, "and fundamentally I am a country man."

Three years before, during a visit in the spring of 1963 to the Ireland his great-grandfather had left as an emigrant, the then President of the United States, John Fitzgerald Kennedy, had spoken in the Dail. Modern Ireland, he had said, as "one of the youngest of nations and the oldest of civilizations, has discovered that the achievement of nationhood is not an end, but a beginning." The American President went on: "In the years since independence, you have undergone a new, peaceful revolution, an economic and industrial revolution . . ."

Kennedy spoke about what might have happened if his great-grandfather had not emigrated to America and if De Valera had never left his birthplace in the United States. "If this nation had achieved its present political and economic structure a century or so ago," Kennedy told the members of the Dail, "my great-grandfather might never have left . . . and I might, if fortunate, be sitting down there with you. Of course, if your own President had never left New York, he might be standing up here, instead of me."

De Valera was pleased, but content to be the President he was, of the nation he had helped create, his own Republic of Ireland.

INDEX

Abyssina, 159
Africa, 67, 76, 129, 175
All-Ireland Council, 69
All-Ireland Parliament, 94
American invasion scare, 164
American Revolution, 66
Appearance, De Valera's physical,
  3, 5, 13, 65, 152–3, 176
Arbour Hill Barracks, 130
Ard-Fheis, first (1917), 50–52
Asgard, the, 15
Ashe, Thomas, 50
Aud, the, 22–3, 24–5, 26
Australia, 168

Bachelor's Walk, 16
Ballsbridge Barracks, 37–9
Barton, Robert, 83, 88, 95–6
Beggars' Bush Barracks, 31–2
Belfast, 11, 12, 16, 58, 77–8, 132
Better Government of Ireland Act,
  69, 74, 75, 143
Birkenhead, Lord, 90, 96
Black-and-Tans, 72–3
Blackrock, 136, 153
Blackrock College, 5–6
Blue Shirt movement, 151–2
Boland, Harry, 60, 125

Boland's Bakery, 31–6
Bonds, Irish Republican, 66–7, 69
Boston, 168
Boundary commission, Ulster, 93,
  94, 131–2, 143
Boyhood, De Valera's, 2–6
British Army conscription, 1918,
  53–4
British Governor-General, 93, 133,
  142, 148–9, 154, 174
British Privy Council, appeals to,
  148
Brugha, Cathal, 51, 55, 61, 62–3,
  74, 85, 91, 93, 99, 111, 112, 120–
  121
Bruree, 2–6
Buckley, Daniel, 149
Burma, 156, 168

California, 67, 68
Canada, 93
Carson, Edward, 11, 12
Carysfort Training College, 6, 9, 24
Casement, Roger, 22–3, 25
Cashel, 6
Celtic, the, 70
Censorship, wartime, 163
Chamberlain, Austen, 90, 96

Chamberlain, Neville, 159–60
Channel Islands, 163
Charleville, 4, 5
Chicago, 67, 168
Chicago Tribune, 111
Childers, Erskine, 15, 83, 88, 125
Chippewa Indian Chief, De Valera
  made, 68
Christian Brothers, 4, 5, 6
Churchill, Winston, 76, 78, 90, 92,
  96, 98, 104, 109, 114, 117, 144,
  160, 161–2, 164–5
Citizens' Army, 13–14, 27
Citizenship, De Valera's, 40, 66
Civil War, Irish, vii, 101–7, 109–30,
  139, 145, 148
Clann na Poblachta, 166
Clanwilliam House, 31–2, 34
Clare, County, 45, 47–8, 49, 58, 75,
  130, 172–3
Clarke, T. J., 39
Cleveland, 68
Clonmel, 123
Coalition government, proposed,
  114–6
Coll, Edmond, 2
Coll, Elizabeth, 2–3
Coll, Patrick, 2, 4
Collins, Michael, 43, 51, 55, 60, 62,
  63, 64, 70, 72, 74, 85, 88, 90,
  92, 93, 94–5, 96, 102–4, 109–10,
  111–13, 114–15, 116–17, 124–5,
  129
Collins-De Valera pact, 111–13,
  114, 115, 125
Colonialism, vi–vii, 40, 67, 76, 77,
  83, 86–7, 129
Colorado, 68
Congo, 175
Congress, United States, 46, 63
Connolly, James, 14, 21, 23, 27, 39,
  42
Constitution, 115, 136, 140, 147,
  148, 154, 155–7, 174, 177

Contarf, 16
Cope, Alfred, 76
Cork, County, 2, 24, 123
Cosgrave, Liam, 176
Cosgrave, William, 49–50, 55, 62,
  88, 91, 124, 126, 127, 129, 130,
  131, 132, 133, 138, 139, 140,
  141, 142, 143, 145, 150, 151–2,
  176
Costello, John, 167–8, 169, 170
Courts, Sinn Fein, 62, 69–70
Craig, Sir James, 11, 75, 77, 79, 82
Cumann na nGaedheal, 138, 142
Cyprus, 175

Dail Eireann, 61, 62–3, 67, 71, 73,
  74–5, 85, 99–100, 101–7, 109,
  111, 112, 113, 115, 124, 126,
  131, 132, 133, 135, 138, 140,
  141, 142, 143, 145, 147, 148,
  150, 154, 169, 170, 178
Daily Express, London, 48
Dartmoor Prison, 40–41
Debt payments to Britain, 132, 133,
  143, 149, 159–60
Declaration of Independence, Irish,
  61
Depression, the, 144, 150
Derby, Lord, 76–7
Derry, 132
DeValera, Ann, 170, 176
De Valera, Brian, 9, 154
De Valera, Eamonn (son), 9, 154
De Valera, Eammon (grandson),
  170
De Valera, Emer, 154
De Valera, Mairin, 9, 153–4
De Valera, Ruairi, 47, 154
De Valera, Sinead, 7–8, 13, 27, 47,
  118, 153, 170, 173
De Valera, Terry, 118, 154
De Valera, Vivion (father), 1–2
De Valera, Vivion (son), 8, 118–9,
  153, 170

De Valera-Lloyd George conferences, 1921, 83, 84, 85
Dillon, John, 58
Dominion status, 76, 77, 83–4, 86–87, 90, 91, 92, 93, 97, 127, 133, 144, 154
Donnybrook, 8, 47
Down, County, 75, 131
Dublin Brigade, 19, 23, 24, 27, 30–36, 119
Dublin Castle, 15, 25, 29, 49, 72, 79, 104, 173, 174
Duffy, Gavan, 88, 95
Duggan, Eamonn, 88, 95, 96
Dunne, Reginald, 116

Easter Rising, the, v, vi, vii, 19–27, 29–36, 37–8, 52, 61, 106, 173
Economic independence, 150
Economic War with Britain, 149–150, 157, 159–60
Edward VIII, 154, 155
Eire, 156
Eisenhower, Dwight, 174
Elections: 1918, 57–9, 61; 1920, 69; 1921, 74–5; 1922, 114–16; 1923, 129–30; June, 1927, 138; September, 1927, 142; 1932, 145; 1933, 150; 1937, 156; 1948, 166; 1951, 1954, 169–70; 1957, 170; 1959, 171; 1966, 176–7
Electoral Amendment Act, 140, 141
Ennis, 172–3
European Economic Community, 175
Executions, 38–40, 42–3, 72, 125–6
External Association, 85–7, 89–92, 93, 95, 96, 99, 154–5, 157, 168
External Relations Act, 154–5, 169
Eyesight, De Valera's, 154, 167

Farmer's Party, 142, 167
Fermoy, 123

Fianna Fail, 135–42, 143, 144–5, 166, 170, 171–2
Fine Gael, 152, 167, 170, 171, 176
Flag, Republican tricolor, 49, 52
Four Courts, occupation of, 110–111, 117–8, 119–20, 125
Free State, Irish, 93, 94, 97, 99, 103–7, 109, 111, 112, 114, 115, 117–20, 123, 124, 125, 126, 127, 128–33, 135–42, 144
French, Field Marshal Lord, 54, 55
Frongoch internment camp, 43

Gaelic Athletic Association, 9
Gaelic language, 3, 6, 7–8, 9, 170, 173
Gaelic League, 7, 8, 9, 12, 19, 157
Gandhi, Indira, 168
General Post Office, Dublin, 23, 29–30, 33, 35, 136, 173
General strike, 1918, 54
George V, 77–9, 96
Germany, 14, 15, 16, 22, 23, 24, 25, 33, 55, 159, 161, 163
Greystones, 47, 55, 118–9
Griffith, Arthur, 10, 16–17, 20–21, 43, 51, 55, 62, 64, 70, 81, 83, 85, 88, 90, 91–2, 93, 94, 95, 96, 102–4 106–7, 109–10, 114–15, 117–18, 124, 129
Gun-running, 14–15, 22–4

Hamman Hotel, 120–21
Harding, Warren, 70
Helga, the, 35
Henry, Patrick, 68
Hitler, 159, 161, 163
Hitzen, Capt. E. J., 36
Home industry, 150
Home Rule, 11, 12, 17, 20, 42, 43, 44, 48, 50, 51, 53–4, 84, 164
Housing program, 150
Howth, 15
Hyde, Douglas, 7, 157

Idaho, 68
Independence Hall, Philadelphia,
     68
India, 67, 76, 156, 168, 175
Irish Press, the, 137, 170
Irish Republican Army, 21, 29–36,
     73–4, 98, 99, 105–7, 123, 124,
     125, 126, 127, 128, 133, 139,
     151–2, 166; see also *Irish Volun-
     teers*.
Irish Republican Brotherhood, 10,
     12, 19, 20–21, 23, 43, 51, 60
Irish Transport and General Work-
     ers Union, 14
Irish Volunteers, 9, 12–13, 14–16,
     17, 19–21, 23–7, 29–36, 41, 45,
     46, 52, 55, 62–3, 71–2, 73, 105–7,
     110–11, 117–18, 119, 120; see
     also *Irish Republican Army*.
Irish War for Independence, 6, 7,
     69, 70, 71–9, 81–2

Jail escape, De Valera's Lincoln,
     59–61
Japan, 159

Kennedy, John F., 178
Kerry, County, 123
Kilkenny, 49
Kilmainham Prison, 38
Kingstown (Dun Laoghaire), 23,
     31, 34, 45, 55

Labor Party, 50, 53, 111, 142, 145,
     167, 170
Land Annuities, 143, 149
Lapland, the, 64
La Scala Theater, 135
Law, Bonar, 12
League of Nations, 144, 158–9, 174
Lebanon, 175
Leinster College of Irish, 7, 8
Lemass, Sean, 171, 173, 177–8

Lewes Jail, 41, 43–4
Liberty Hall, 14, 26, 33
Limerick, County, 1–6, 24
Lincoln Jail, 55, 57, 58–60, 61
Lindbergh, Charles, 167
Lloyd George, 42, 44, 50, 52–3, 57,
     66, 69, 71, 73, 75–6, 77–9, 81–5,
     86–8, 90–91, 92–3, 95–8, 115
Lynch, Jack, 178
Lynch, Liam, 123, 125, 127
Lynch, Patrick, 48

Mac Bride, Sean, 166
Mac Donagh, Thomas, 19, 21, 23,
     25, 27, 39
Mac Eoin, Sean, 171
Mc Guinness, Joseph, 44
Mac Neill, Eoin, 12, 20, 23, 24,
     25–6, 41, 62, 130
Mac Neill, James, 148
Macready, Gen. Nevil, 117
Madison Square Garden, 67
Maidstone Jail, 41
Maigue, River, 2
Manchester, 60
Manchuria, 159
Mansion House, 50, 61, 81–2
Markievicz, Countess Constance,
     62
Maxwell, Gen. Sir John, 35, 38
Mayo, County, 58
Middle East, 175
Montana, 67
Mount Street Bridge, 31, 34
Mulcahy, Richard, 62, 63, 106–7,
     125–6
Mussolini, 151

National Coalition Government,
     proposed, 112–13, 115–16
Nazi invasion threat, 161, 163–64
Negotiations, Irish-British 1921
     peace, 77–9, 81–3

Nehru, Premier, 168
Neutrality, Irish, 16–17, 150, 159–160, 161–5
New England, 66
New Hampshire, 66
New Jersey, 68
New York, 1, 64, 65, 67, 167–8
Normandy, 164
Northern Ireland, 10–12, 17, 42, 58, 69, 74–5, 77–8, 81–2, 84, 94, 105, 110, 114, 127, 129, 131–2, 133, 155, 156, 161, 164, 165, 167–8, 169

Oath to the King, 84, 91, 93, 95, 97, 98, 104, 114, 115–16, 125, 127, 129, 131, 132, 133, 135, 138, 140–1, 142, 144, 147, 148, 154
O'Casey, Sean, 8
O'Connell, Gen. "Ginger," 118
O'Connor, Rory, 106–7, 110–11, 117, 118, 120, 125
O'Duffy, Eoin, 151–2
O'Higgins, Kevin, 124, 130, 139–40
O'Higgins, T. F., 176, 177
O'Kelly, Sean, 172
O'Neill, Lord Mayor, 111

Pakistan, 156, 175
Parliamentary Party, 11, 48, 53–4, 58
Partition of Ireland, 10, 11–12, 17, 30, 42, 69, 77–8, 81–2, 86, 91, 92, 94, 98, 127, 129, 131–3, 136, 143, 154, 156, 161, 167–8, 169, 170
Peace conference, Versailles, 58–9, 60, 63–4, 87–8
Pearse, Margaret, 137
Pearse, Patrick, 19–20, 24, 25, 26, 30–31, 33, 35, 37, 39, 42
Pearse, William, 39
Peat industry, 150

Pentonville Prison, 44–5
Philadelphia, 65, 68, 168
Phoenix Park, 148–9, 154, 174, 175
Plunkett, Count, 43, 62
Plunkett, Joseph, 43
Postwar recovery, 165–6, 177
President's House, 175, 176, 178
Proclamation of Irish Republic, 24, 30–31, 43, 61
Proportional representation, 172

Reading habits, De Valera's, 4, 5, 153, 176
Redmond, John, 11, 12, 17, 43
Republic of Ireland Act, 168–9
Reynolds, George, 31
Richmond, Va., 68
Richmond Barracks, 38, 39
Rochester, N.Y., 5, 65, 137
Rockwell College, 6
Roosevelt, Franklin D., 152, 164
Roscommon, 43
Royal Irish Constabulary, 72

Schooling, De Valera's, 3, 4–6
Shaw, George Bernard, 39
Simpson, Mrs. Ernest, 154
Sinn Fein, 9–10, 16, 20, 43, 44, 45, 48, 49–50, 51, 52, 53, 54, 55, 57–59, 61, 62, 69, 74–6, 91, 93, 110, 112–13, 114, 115, 129–33, 135, 138–9
Smuts, Jan Christiaan, 77, 78
Soldier's Song, The, 38, 45, 173
South Africa, Union of, 175
Southern Rhodesia, 175
Sovereignty, Irish people's, 81, 86, 87, 89, 91, 127, 142, 147, 154, 158–9
Soviet Union, 174
Spooner, Wisc., 68
Sports, 3–4, 5, 6, 49, 153, 176

Stack, Austin, 74, 83, 85, 91, 93, 99, 120

Statute of Westminster, 144, 147

Stock market crash, 1929 New York, 144

Stowaway, De Valera as a, 64, 70

Sunday Independent, the, 26

Teaching career, De Valera's, 5–8, 24, 153

Third Battalion, Volunteer, 23, 24, 27, 31, 45, 119

Thomas, James, 147, 149

Times, the London, 58

Tipperary, County, 6, 24, 63, 123, 127

Treaty conferences, Irish-British, 83–5, 86–8, 89–100, 101–2

Treaty ports, Irish, 133, 142, 157–8, 159–60, 164

Tricolor flag, Republican, 30, 33, 173

Trinity College, 29, 33

Truce, Irish-British 1921, 82–3

Truman, Harry, 168

Ulster, 10–12, 14, 15, 16, 17, 42, 58, 69, 74–5, 77–8, 81–2, 84, 91, 92, 94, 114, 131–2, 133, 169

Ultimatum, British treaty, 96–7

Unemployment relief, 150

Union Party, 11, 58, 75, 77–8, 82, 114, 169

United Nations, 174–5

United States, De Valera's visits to, 1919–20, 63–4, 65–70; 1927, 137; 1948, 167–8

Utah, 67

Vice-Regal Lodge, 148–9, 174

Victoria, Queen, 174

Walsh, Archbishop, 111

Washington, D.C., 22, 42, 63

Waterford, County, 123, 127

Westland Row Station, 31, 45

Wexford, County, 123

Wheat shortage, 150

Wheelwright, Catherine Coll De Valera, 1–2, 5, 65, 137

Wheelwright, Charles, 5

Wicklow, County, 47

Wilson, Sir Henry, 114, 116–17

Wilson, Woodrow, 46, 50, 58–9, 60, 63, 64, 66, 69, 70, 87–8

World Appeal Against Partition, 167–8

World tour, De Valera's 1948, 167–8

World unrest, De Valera on causes of, 158–9

World War I, 14, 16, 17, 20, 21–22, 23, 40, 42, 46, 48, 53–4, 57, 61, 63–4

World War II, 150, 157, 159, 160, 161–5